JUNIOR
MARTIAL
ARTS

C000088799

**Other martial arts books
available from A & C Black:**

Elite Karate Techniques (David Mitchell)
Health and Fitness in the Martial Arts
    (Dr J. C. Canney)
Judo Games (Geof Gleeson)
Judo Inside out (Geof Gleeson)
Know the Game Judo (Geof Gleeson)
Know the Game Karate (Martial Arts
    Commission)
The Martial Arts Coaching Manual (David
    Mitchell)
Okinawan Karate (Mark Bishop)
Self Defence for All (Fay Goodman)
Skilful Karate (Greg McLatchie)

JUNIOR MARTIAL ARTS

TONY GUMMERSON

A & C Black · London

First published 1990 by
A & C Black (Publishers) Limited
35 Bedford Row, London WC1R 4JH

© 1990 Tony Gummerson

ISBN 0–7136–5697–2

All rights reserved. No part of this publication
may be reproduced, stored in a retrieval system,
or transmitted in any form or by any means,
electronic, mechanical, photocopying, recording
or otherwise, without the prior permission in
writing of A & C Black (Publishers) Limited

A CIP catalogue record for this book is
available from the British Library

Typeset by Latimer Trend & Company Ltd, Plymouth
Printed and bound in Great Britain by
BPCC Hazell Books
Member of BPCC Ltd.
Aylesbury, Bucks, England

Contents

ACKNOWLEDGEMENTS

For the preparation of this book I am indebted to several individuals who have influenced my thinking on the training of junior martial artists. Of particular importance have been:

Dr James Canney, Medical Officer of the Martial Arts Commission, who has done much to identify the specific training requirements of junior students; *David Mitchell*, who has created an interest in the development of coaching throughout all the martial arts, and who was the prime mover in the implementation of the current M.A.C. Coach Education Programme; members of the B.J.J.A.—Allan Campbell, for his technical assistance, and David, Steven, Carl and Jonathan for their modelling expertise.

INTRODUCTION

A recent survey conducted by the Martial Arts Commission of Great Britain suggested that as many as 60% of all practising martial artists in the United Kingdom were under 16 years of age. It would appear that the martial arts are following the trend of most sports and recreational activities in Great Britain and, I suspect, the rest of the world where the majority of participants are teenagers. However, few of the martial arts associations and governing bodies have a specific syllabus for youngsters, despite the fact that most of their members fall into this age category.

This seems to be a strange state of affairs when as far back as 1977 the Health Education Council of Great Britain saw the need to give young people a basic knowledge of the benefits of physical exercise. It further suggested that youngsters should be given the opportunity to understand that exercise can help to maintain muscles, joints, heart and lungs in good condition. This recommendation is fully supported by the view of the World Health Organisation which states that the prevention of disease has become a priority and that exercise is a vital element in the process. The martial arts, therefore, have an important role to play in the development of a good attitude towards physical activity, not only as an end in itself (in the learning of techniques) but in the hope that the understanding of the importance of exercise at an early age will last in to adulthood. Further recent research has shown that any physical benefits gained early on will have a continued and positive bearing on general health throughout life.

The purpose of this book is to look at the very specific needs, both physical and psychological, of the young martial artist. It has to be clearly understood that young martial arts students are not 'little adults'. The training, grading and competition which are appropriate to the senior students may not be relevant to or suitable for the younger ones. The opportunities which martial arts can offer young students, together with the correct approach to training and assessment, will be clearly identified.

The book is divided into two sections. In the first part the main aspects of physical growth and intellectual development, and their importance in the appropriate, systematic and progressive development of young students are discussed. This is not too academic in nature, being aimed at the 'practical' coach.

In the second section the specific application of theory in practice is described. This aims to give the coach an insight into how theory can be applied in the training situation. The development of the essential elements of martial arts techniques is shown, as well as ways in which coaches can make activities more specific and appropriate to their own martial art or style. Finally, a suggestion of possible assessment and grading activities is included to help both coaches and students measure the rate of development and progress.

Throughout the book students and coaches are, in the main, referred to individually as 'he'. This should, of course, be taken to mean 'he or she' where appropriate.

A BASIC PHILOSOPHY

It is, of course, true to say that there have been and always will be examples of outstanding performance in teenage, or even younger, sportsmen and women. Though excellent performance may be the essence of a coach's training programme, it should be seen as part of the long-term development of a student both as a martial artist and as a member of society. Participation in any physical activity at an early age, though enjoyable and healthy in itself, is the foundation for continued and progressive involvement into adulthood and physical and mental maturity (see fig. 1).

Adaptation

Training brings about specific adaptations of individual students' bodies to the type of activities repeatedly practised. To have the best effect any training programme must take into account the mechanisms through which the body adapts. When compared with the adult, the young student responds to the

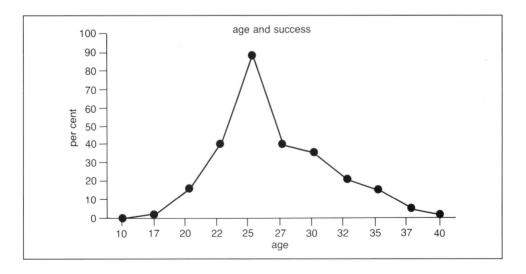

Fig. 1   The age at which most sportsmen and women achieve sporting success at international levels is between 20 and 30 years.

same training regime in a different manner. This is because body changes, as a result of training, depend on the state of development of various body organs and systems. It is quite clear, therefore, that training methods used to produce excellence in adults may not be the most efficient or appropriate to develop a similar standard in youngsters.

Martial arts training will obviously bring about the development of skills and techniques while at the same time it will develop students' general level of fitness. In fact, the two aspects go hand in hand: the development of fitness will improve the learning and refinement of techniques, while at the same time the very activity of practising techniques over a period of time will be beneficial in improving specific aspects of fitness.

In summary, medical advice indicates that some form of physical activity started at an early age may act as a preventative for future health problems. So, teaching good habits of regular, well-designed physical exercise is an essential aspect of the young martial artist's training. It is essential, therefore, that carefully designed programmes are devised for young students, programmes not only relevant to their particular stage of maturation but which keep an eye on the future and the long-term benefits of regular exercise and good health.

GROWTH

Growth might be described as 'the progressive and continuous development of an individual through both the structure and function of organs and body systems'. This process continues until all these elements are fully developed and a state of 'maturity' is established. However, this must not be confused with the *potential* of an individual which is dependent on two main factors.

Genetics

Inherited characteristics from both parents determine an individual's potential capacity for development.

Environment

The life style in which an individual is raised can affect growth. Correct nutrition, healthy living conditions, a caring home environment, stable and positive social and emotional relationships all affect the rate of maturation.

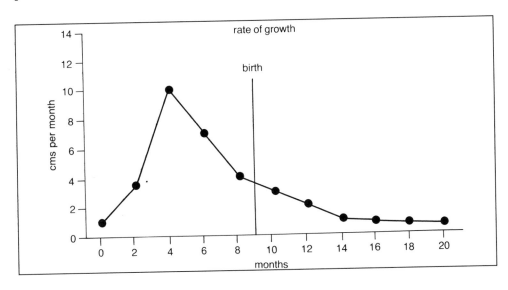

Fig. 2   The period of maximum rate of growth is three months after conception.

Genetic inheritance identifies the potential that an individual might achieve. However, this will only be reached if the environmental aspects are conducive to growth. For example, a poor diet will not allow for maximum tissue growth because the nutrients either are not there or are not present in the correct amounts. It can be seen, therefore, that without the right environment an individuals potential might never fully be realised.

The growth of an individual and the development of various organs are not constant. The fastest rate of growth occurs before birth, approximately 3 months after conception (see fig. 2). Thereafter a relatively steady and uniform period of development continues from birth until the stage of development known as 'puberty' is reached. At this time, somewhere between 11–13 years in girls and 13–15 in boys, there is a noticeable acceleration of growth known as the 'adolescent growth spurt' (see fig. 3).

PUBERTY

The changes taking place during this period of rapid growth are the direct result of the release of increased amounts of hormones. These are mainly from the pituitary glands, and from the ovaries in females and the testes in males.

In males the testes produce levels of the male sex hormone **testosterone**. Changes characteristic of male adolescence are subsequently brought about.

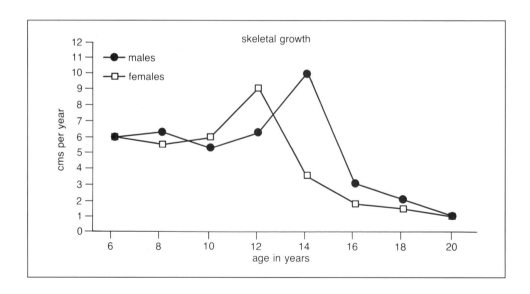

Fig. 3   The difference in growth rates between boys and girls at puberty can clearly be seen.

These are:

- growth of facial and body hair
- enlargement of the larynx, leading to a deepening of the voice
- growth of the reproductive organs
- development of sex drive
- bone growth
- muscle growth
- development of aggression.

In females the ovaries produce increased levels of the female sex hormones **oestrogen** and **progesterone**. Changes characteristic of female adolescence are subsequently produced. These are:

- growth of pubic hair
- development of breasts
- onset of menstruation
- development of sex drive
- bone growth }
- muscle growth } not as much as in males.

It is obvious from personal observation that children mature at different rates and so there are going to be considerable variations in the timing of the adolescent growth spurt. Therefore, chronological age is not an accurate enough measurement of physiological maturity. Usually the rate of ossification of growing bone (the rate at which bone becomes hard) as identified by X-rays, or the development of the teeth, are used, certainly by the medical world, as being a more accurate assessment of the rate or stage of maturation. Such techniques are not readily available to the average coach!

During the growth spurt period there appear to be clearly identified phases of development. The sequence of growth seems to follow the following pattern.

- *Phase one:* growth of leg length.
- *Phase two:* development of body 'width'.
- *Phase three:* development of trunk length.
- *Phase four:* muscle growth (this follows the peak period of skeletal and organ growth).

AGE, MATURATION AND PERFORMANCE

Strength

There appears to be very little difference in strength levels between boys and girls before puberty (see fig. 4). In activities requiring strength and power, girls

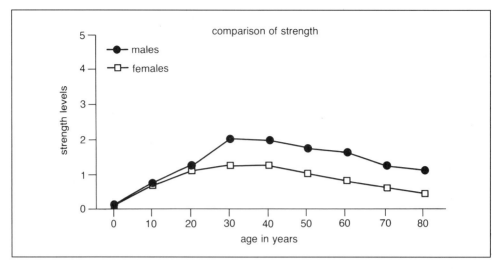

Fig. 4   The difference in strength levels between boys and girls is minimal up to puberty. After that, males have a natural advantage.

are more or less on equal terms with boys of the same age. During puberty and after, however, there is a rapid improvement in the strength of males. In females any improvement is far less obvious.

The significant difference between the sexes after puberty seems to correspond with the development of upper body strength. It has been noted that in males the increase in strength seems to surpass any other developmental

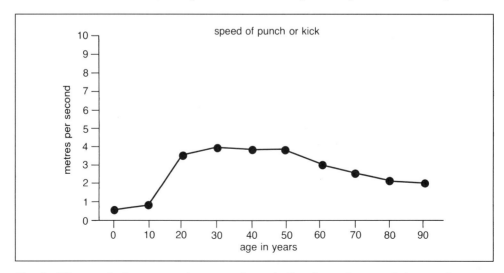

Fig. 5   The speed of movement improves dramatically after puberty and then tends to plateau, falling rapidly after 50.

change. There is a period of approximately 12 months for strength levels to 'catch up' with skeletal changes, and there seems to be an increase in muscle size which precedes the development of strength.

Speed

After the age of about 3 there seems to be no increase in the rate at which nerve fibres transmit information. Any advance in the rate of signals being passed from the brain to the rest of the body appears to depend on the brain's development in processing information. This maturational process can be identified with the rapid development of systems around puberty, particularly body co-ordination.

'Motor co-ordination' develops sharply from about the age of 5. Thereafter a steadier rate of increase occurs until puberty when once again there is a rapid increase. Up to about the age of 13 there is little difference between the sexes; afterwards there is a greater increase in co-ordination in boys than in girls.

As to the speed of movement of the whole body, or of a limb, this is dependent on the rate of muscular contraction and the range of movement through which the muscle moves (see fig. 5). Until puberty there is no muscle fibre differentiation in that there are no fast contracting fibres (see fig. 6). Figure 7 shows the contribution of the different fibre types to the different

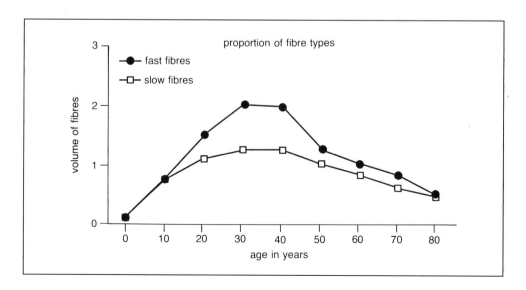

Fig. 6   Fibre differentiation occurs after puberty when fast fibres develop. Their numbers peak in individuals of around 30 years, but these fall dramatically after the age of 40.

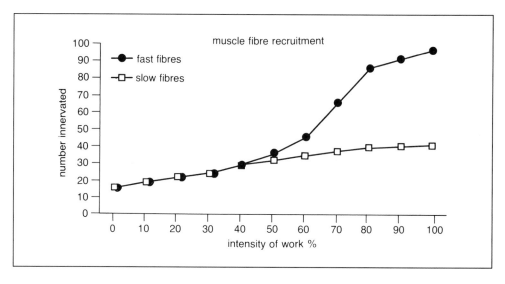

Fig. 7   The presence of fast fibres is essential where the work rate exceeds 50% of maximum.

As the intensity increases, so does the contribution of the fast contracting fibres to the total muscular force produced.

intensities of work. Furthermore, until puberty there is little muscle strength to influence speed of body/limb movement. Also, because of immature skeletal development, there are no long levers to influence rate of movement in a negative or a positive fashion. It should be noted, however, that because of the delicate nature of bone and connective tissue the forces generated in movements at speed offer potentially very dangerous situations.

Endurance

Basically, the youngster is an aerobic animal. However, as mentioned earlier, there is no muscle fibre differentiation prior to puberty, although aerobic-type muscle fibres are present in abundance. As with all growing tissue, part of the function of aerobic muscle fibres is to develop the ability to tolerate fatigue. Therefore, intense training will be limited. The build-up of waste products in active muscle can cause problems, requiring regular periods of rest to allow for their removal.

Very intense or anaerobic activity poses specific difficulties for the young martial artist: he does not possess the appropriate type of muscle fibre required for such activity, and his body systems are not geared to such demands of energy production or to the rapid removal of their waste products (see fig. 8). This means that periods of low work intensity will be much better for him than

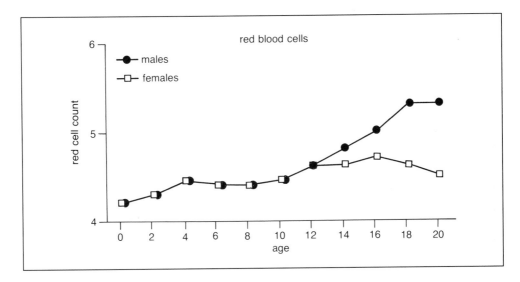

Fig. 8   The number of red blood cells (which are crucial in the transport of oxygen) increases dramatically after puberty. Note the difference between males and females.

shorter periods of high intensity activity. Any intensive training is going to bring about rapid fatigue and a relatively long period of recovery will be needed to allow for the removal of fatigue products (see fig. 9).

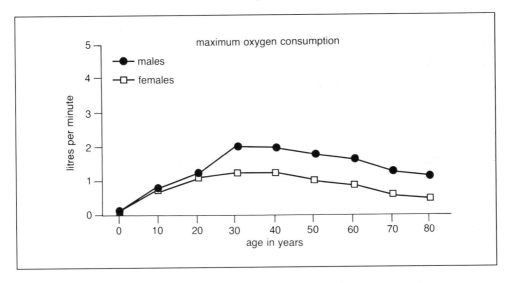

Fig. 9   The total amount of oxygen which the body can take in per minute is directly related to the amount of work that can be done. The more oxygen available, the greater the quantity and quality of work. Note the big increase after puberty. Compare the graph with Fig. 8.

Mobility

Connective tissue in children is elastic. Youngsters, by and large, are very mobile individuals. However, one must be aware of the danger that over-stretching connective tissue might pose. Ligaments are generally responsible for maintaining the alignment of bone with bone at joints. Overstretching elastic ligaments could cause bones to become misaligned, thereby creating difficulties. Similarly, stresses placed on tendons and ligaments can aggravate their junction with bones, causing all kinds of inflammatory conditions. So, it has to be remembered that it is possible to develop natural mobility at the risk of either overuse type injuries or far more serious structural damage which may not manifest itself until later life.

LEARNING THE SKILLS

The past decade has seen much research into the importance and effect of physical activity on children. Often, however, what has emerged are programmes of training and skill development for adults which have been 'watered down' for youngsters. However, out of these studies has emerged a general pattern of motor and specific skill learning (see fig. 10). It must be realised that there is an almost parallel growth of physiological and psychological elements in the youngster. These are interwoven in any general or specific physical movement or technique. It therefore follows that there has to be a carefully designed programme of martial art technique and skill learning which corresponds with the developmental level of the individual.

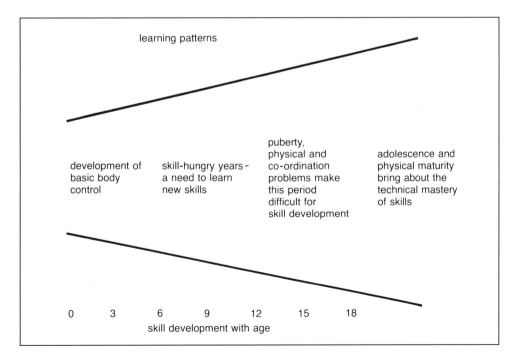

Fig. 10 A simplistic view of the development of the learning patterns as the youngster grows towards maturity.

Motor learning

There is evidence to support the notion of four broad areas of motor learning.

Reflex movements

From birth and even, according to some experts, before birth, the individual is evolving basic reflex type movements. These tend to be basic postural movements, especially of the head, neck and back, as well as experiments in moving limbs by flexing and extending joints. The infant is generally exploring his body and his ability to interact with his immediate surroundings. As sight, hearing, touch and balance improve, together with physical and intellectual capacity, more demanding skills are performed, such as sitting, reaching and grasping, crawling, standing and walking. These more advanced skills in turn allow the infant to experience more stimuli from the world around him and so create the foundation for further intellectual and physical growth. A certain level of development is attained by the time the individual is about 2 years old, although to stick rigidly to chronological age can be misleading as some youngsters will obviously improve at a more rapid rate than others. However, generally speaking, by the age of 2 this level of attainment can be expected.

Communication

As speech develops, so too does the ability of the infant to communicate with the world in general. He is able to talk to others and to express likes, dislikes and ideas. Furthermore, he can listen to new ideas and absorb information as part of the learning process. Walking progresses into running; the development of judgement allows for variations in speed. Jumping and landing skills improve, as do applied movements, such as turning, bending, stretching, twisting, pushing and pulling activities. The individual becomes more aware of his body and how it moves and is able to co-ordinate its movement with intellectual reasoning in play and games. More complex skills which depend upon the integration of mind and body in a highly co-ordinated fashion evolve, for example, throwing, punching, patting and kicking, as well as catching and evasion techniques. These fundamental patterns of movement and perceptual awareness are generally established by the age of eight.

Development of co-ordination

From the age of eight movement patterns can be expanded and refined, mainly because the individual is aware of the position of his body or of the 'feel' of a movement. This allows him to modify an action as required. Also, very importantly, the youngster can appreciate intellectually the quality of movement and can understand what is needed. The skills learned in the previous stages act as the foundation for the new and specific ones introduced from now on. General patterns of movement are applied in specific activities and games. This level of development is usually attained by the age of 12 years.

Specialisation

From the age of 12 the application of skills develops, as do intellectual and reasoning powers. There tends to be much more specialisation into specific sports or activities in which the individual is interested. With the onset of puberty and the approach of adulthood there is a great change not only in the physical make-up of the youngster but also in behavioural, emotional, sociological and intellectual ways as well. Physical activity becomes more important as exercise, leisure and recreation. Other values, such as those relating to competition, social interaction, attainment and making friends begin to be formed.

The sequence of these developmental stages is progressive in that the skills learned in one phase are the foundation for refinement into more complex ones in the next. It is very difficult, if not impossible, to teach individuals skills or techniques appropriate to their developmental stage if they have not experienced, let alone mastered, the previous ones.

The evolution of skills seems to follow a progressive pattern. In chronological order these are:

- an awareness of being alive
- an awareness of one's body, limbs and movement
- an awareness of one's physical situation and place within the environment
- an awareness of up, down, left, right and combinations of direction
- an awareness of time present, future and past
- an awareness of tempo and rhythm
- an awareness of co-ordinating hand and foot movements with vision.

There is also a general development of the senses:

- vision
- hearing
- touch
- balance
- smell
- taste.

As the basic senses improve and the body begins to grow, these elements can be incorporated into the refinement of slightly more complex skills:

- reaching
- grasping
- sitting
- crawling
- standing
- falling
- walking
- running with variations of pace and style
- jumping with variations in take-off
- landing with variations of feet positions
- rolling
- climbing.

As these movement skills develop there is a need for greater intellectual involvement. This is particularly the case when selecting the correct movement pattern in response to a given situation, such as

- pushing
- pulling
- spinning
- twisting
- bending
- stretching.

Once again, these body movements provide a platform for learning more complex skills which require co-ordination between the whole body and particular parts of it. These skills include:

- throwing
- punching
- patting
- bouncing
- kicking
- catching
- trapping objects with the feet.

The martial arts coach has to face a fundamental problem from the outset. Techniques used in martial arts were designed mainly by men and for use by men in the conflict situation. It is assumed that individuals each have a measure of strength, speed, endurance and mobility as a basis on which specific skills can be learned. It does not require much insight to realise that youngsters do not possess these elements of fitness to the same degree as an an adult. Furthermore, how can a coach hope to teach seven-year-olds complex techniques (let alone their application which requires a high level of intellectual maturity) when they are only just developing the elemental skills of learning how to use their body in a co-ordinated fashion? Before any complex skills can be taught the foundation of basic body movements has to be established. Simplistically, a child who cannot push or throw a ball is going to have difficulty in, for example, the much more complex technique of punching.

THE PSYCHOLOGICAL DIMENSION

A recent study has revealed that over 90% of youngsters in sport want it to be fun, whereas less than 10% have the desire and need to win. The difficulty, of course, is trying to keep an activity fun at the same time as attempting to create an effective learning situation. Studies have identified several aspects of training which have reduced the fun element.

Lessons that are too long

Young students require a 'pace' to a lesson to keep their interest. A constant stream of different techniques and activities is needed. Bearing in mind that lessons usually last between one-and-a-half to two hours, my opinion is that one hour is long enough. From the physiological side, too, one hour's training will develop techniques and fitness elements, but will not cause damage and injury.

Paralysis through analysis

Martial arts are, by definition, highly technical. However, it can be distracting to youngsters if they are constantly corrected. Over-coaching—picking up on every aspect of technique and demanding perfect performance each time— might be appropriate to the adult, but is not appreciated by juniors who simply want 'to get on with it!' The very complexity of some of the linked techniques and katas can also be a barrier to many students.

Teaching methods that are too formal

A rigid, overbearing lesson structure can be a definite turn off for a young student who would respond better to being treated in a less clinical, personal fashion. However, this ideal must obviously be looked at in the light of the nature of the martial art and its intrinsic philosophy and need for safety in practice.

Too much emphasis on success

According to most medical thought on the matter, children have no sense of value. They have it thrust upon them by parents, coaches, advisers or anyone else who is in a position to influence them. And, have no doubt about it, they are both very susceptible to suggestion and easily influenced by adults' comments. Too often, young students are affected by the personal frustrations of coach and parent. They are seen as a means by which success can be achieved.

The notions of determination, having a will to win and competitive spirit are often superimposed, possibly unwittingly, upon the normal values of the youngster. However, they expose the young martial artist to many pressures. When success becomes the only aim, failure to achieve excellence can produce a sense of guilt. The feeling of letting down both parents and coach, as well as oneself, can markedly affect the attitude of the performer. Youngsters like to please and if they don't, they feel guilty and as though they have failed. Such a situation is totally unwarranted.

Competition

This leads on to the thorny question of the place of competition for juniors in the martial arts. Does the desire to compete come from the student, or from the parents/coaches who see their protégés as a means to self-aggrandisement or advancement. I'm sure some of you will have heard the comment, 'I've won three championship titles today' as the coach talks about his young students. Who is using whom? The fact that the student may become so disillusioned with the sport after the competition that he leaves soon after is of no consequence.

The 'traditionalist' who does not advocate the sporting element has a problem, too. What is grading but a way of categorising or assessing the ability of an individual in just the same fashion as competition? The truth is that we all respond to success in a favourable way; no one likes failure, especially young students. The real problem would seem to be handling stress well. In a competition which nationally might involve a thousand students only one can win. The other 999 so-called 'failures', however, are equally worthy in their own way. The philosophy of martial arts is that each and every individual should be allowed to achieve that which he is capable of, both in terms of technical and personal development. Though competition has its place, putting too much emphasis on it can have a negative effect.

There is another notion that is often put forward to support the competitive nature of martial arts: 'Competition is an essential aspect of life. You have to learn to compete, how to be successful and how to handle defeats.' Which child said that? I have also heard, 'Children are naturally competitive' (one or two elite, gifted performers might be, but they are in the minority) and, 'Sport is all about winning' (in that case there are more losers than winners).

These ideas seem to identify a misunderstanding of the place of sport or physical activity in the lives of students. There is, however, an even more debatable proposition which has been put forward for the training of young students.

Specialisation

'To get to the top you have to start early.' There are several flaws in this very dangerous assumption which, again, is made by many adults. Firstly, the drop-out rate of youngsters who are pushed into competitive sport is fantastically high. Very few are successful in their age group championships year after year and progress into the adult ranks at the same level of proficiency. In athletics, for example, 2,500 athletes under the age of 18 attended a National Schools Championships and fewer than 10 went on to represent their country. Whatever happened to the other 2,490 who were lost to the sport? Other activities which have similar competitive structures for certain age groups have identified the same problem. It does not follow that because a student is successful at an early age he will continue at that level into adulthood. In fact, often the reverse is true; students specialising in an activity later in life, at around 16, seem to achieve more success and stay in their sport longer than younger children.

Secondly, it is unsound practice to specialise in terms of training too soon. As we have seen, too much specific training can overload young limbs, joints and body systems. Development might lead to early success, but at what price? How many young students have injuries or complain about constant injuries to knees and back? Why do they have these injuries at such a young age?

Coaches and parents have to walk a very difficult path. Whereas they can offer the facilities for the development of each and every student, no matter what their ability, they also have to be able to identify and encourage those who want to achieve excellence. We often do not give youngsters sufficient credit for an understanding of their own abilities. They have a tremendous sense of fair play and a grasp of their own level of ability. In other words, they know how good they are and they are also aware of the pressures under which they are put by overenthusiastic coaches and parents. However, they are not mature enough emotionally to cope with such pressures. How often have juniors fled the mat in floods of tears after a poor performance in competition or grading? Why are they upset? Who have they let down? It is not a 'life or death' situation; youngsters must participate in martial arts because they want to.

DESIGNING THE TRAINING PROGRAMME

By now it should be clear that the learning and teaching of martial arts are dependent on the developmental stage of the student, and on his degree of success in mastering the various elements. Acquisition of skills is related to physical and psychological maturity, these two elements being at all stages closely interdependent.

Physical factors

Work loads

Young martial artists have vital organs, such as the heart and lungs, muscles and bones which are still growing. The difficulty for the coach is to select a suitable work load which will allow them to adapt to specific types of training without causing any structural damage to the body. Indeed, there is evidence to suggest that well-designed training programmes can positively encourage the development of body systems which will have a long-term beneficial effect on general health and well being into later life.

Overuse

Overloading joints and muscles can bring about very quickly the incidence of 'overuse injuries' and, in the extreme cases, can cause serious structural damage. The main difficulty here is that it might be years before the damage is fully recognised.

Training and recovery

There has to be a careful balance between training and recovery so that the various body systems can cope with the effects of training at the same time as continuing to grow.

Repetition

Any activity that tires a student to a point that will not allow repetition of the exercise 'comfortably' is not advisable. In other words, do not overstress the student with too great a training load.

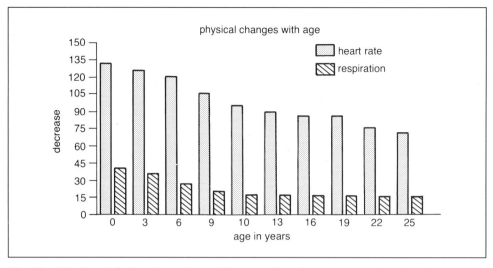

Fig. 11   Figs 8 and 9 show how the working capacity of a student is related to the amount of oxygen available. The picture is made more confusing when the heart rate, which is responsible for circulating blood, and the rate of breathing, which affects the extraction of oxygen, both decline during the same period.

Body conditioning

A general programme of conditioning the body is the foundation for progression to specialisation in particular activities and techniques.

Care of the spine

Very great care must be taken not to overload the spine, either by performing squatting-type activities or by using weights.

Mobility

Mobility exercises designed to maintain and/or increase range of movement must be linked to strengthening activities which will stabilise the specific joint/s.

Work rate

Because of their developmental stage, heart rate is not a good indicator of work rate in young students. Heart rate falls gradually throughout life as the demands placed upon the body decrease (see fig. 11). In youngsters there is a high demand for building materials to allow growth to take place and so heart rate is higher than later in life.

In addition, the lack of differentiation of muscle fibres means that anaerobic work is not readily accepted. The duration of such activity should be short

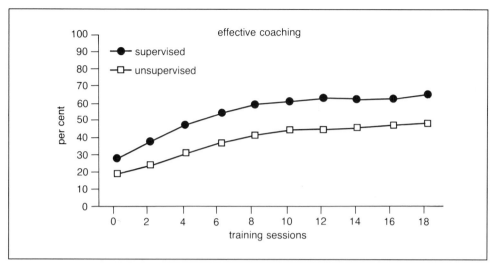

Fig. 12   Practice will improve performance, but it will be much better under the control of a qualified coach.

(the effect upon the heart can seem quite demanding), although there is a tendency for low rates of intensity to be followed by a seemingly disproportionate recovery time. This is where heart rate fails to be a good indicator of intensity of work and recovery. The student should be able to work for at least 20 minutes constantly at low levels of intensity before any intensive anaerobic activity is introduced.

Diet

A well-balanced and varied diet is essential for the young student both for normal growth and for the extra demands of training. A tendency for food fads and a liking for what is referred to as 'junk' food can pose problems.

Psychological factors

It is difficult to separate totally the physical from the psychological, and it should be remembered that the high levels of hormones circulating around the body not only influence the body but the mind as well. The caring coach will readily notice the changes in behaviour in the pre- and post-pubertal student.

Learning techniques correctly

Effective teaching methods must be used, including explanation, demonstration, films, videos and books. It is essential that the correct techniques are taught from the very beginning (see fig. 12). Since skills become 'grooved in' and bring about physical changes in the neuro-muscular system, any errors are very difficult to correct at a later stage. Any faults in techniques must be identified early on so that the cause can be identified, corrected and good practice maintained.

Small groups

The young student tends to work better in small groups where he can receive more attention than if he were in a large impersonal group. This should be closely linked to individual coaching.

Skill learning

For physical and psychological developmental reasons girls between about 8–11 years and boys between 9–12 years are 'skill hungry'. They seem to have an insatiable appetite for learning new physical skills in a number of activities. The difficulty is in the fact that they are soon satisfied with a crude reproduction of a technique and quickly want to move on to the next (see fig. 13).

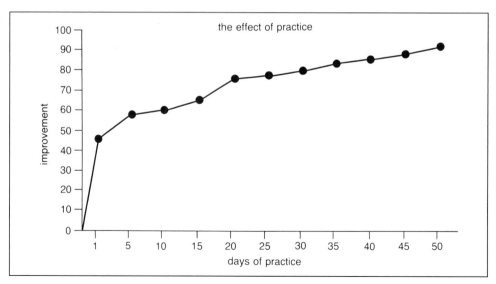

Fig. 13   With the learning of any skill there is a rapid initial improvement. Thereafter, improvement comes more slowly.

Lesson planning

Because of their desire always to be trying new activities, it can be very difficult to keep the attention of young students, particularly when the instructor's aim is to refine a specific technique. The concentration span of a young student is very limited unless the coach can create a dynamic learning situation to maintain his interest. Good planning for training programmes is therefore essential.

Speed

Speed of movement is a characteristic of a highly refined technique. It therefore goes hand in hand with skill development. However, the caring coach will also be aware of the possible dangers in either working at speed or using bad technique (putting joints and connective tissue at risk), or even using a combination of the two.

Social pressures

Young students at this point in time have to cope with tremendous social and psychological pressures in their life. The dojo can provide a wonderful opportunity to leave them all outside the door; it should not be an opportunity to add to them! The caring coach will take into account all the difficulties which a student is facing at home, at school, with friends and in the dojo to create a happy learning experience.

Planning the programme

With these psychological and physical constraints in mind, the coach has to set about designing an appropriate training regime. This will follow certain principles.

General conditioning

The student should work towards sound all-round development of mobility, strength, endurance and a modicum of speed as a foundation for those very specific demands and requirements of advanced techniques. Furthermore, the well conditioned student will be able to get the most out of a training session if he can participate fully. A poorly conditioned student who has to spend a great amount of time resting is not making the best use of the practice or expertise available.

Developing technique

It is essential for instructors to teach good techniques that are appropriate to the developmental stage of individuals. They should also allow for physical and psychological limitations.

Specific conditioning

As more advanced techniques are introduced it is important that specific areas of training, such as strength building, continue to be developed.

Stabilising advanced techniques

It is no good only occasionally being able to reproduce a technically sophisticated technique. The programme must allow for such activities to be practised in an environment conducive to their development. A student and coach must expect all techniques learned to be performed at will with a degree of confidence and should not depend on good fortune.

TRAINING

Programmes

Training programmes designed by a coach for young students will naturally reflect the coach's own personal values. Some coaches see large numbers of students achieving success in major competitions and gradings as being a measure of their own personal ability as instructors. There are other coaches who view the personal development of students as valuable members of society as being more important than pushing them to the very limit of their physical, psychological and emotional abilities.

Recent research has highlighted one of the anomalies of youngsters being involved in sport. The findings indicate that young sportsmen and women can indeed be pushed very hard to gain success at the highest possible level. However, there is usually a price to pay. Injuries are very common, leading not only to a high drop-out rate at the time they occur, but also to physical difficulties in later life. Furthermore, few of the 'elite' students stay in sport. Whether this is due to boredom, staleness or accumulated fatigue is difficult to know.

The study also showed that those youngsters who start late in sport or who are not subject to intensive regimes have fewer injuries and stay longer in the activity than their peers who train hard regularly (see fig. 14). They even achieve, by and large, the same level of success in terms of standard of performance. Which is to be preferred: an excellence in competition and a high turnover of students, or students developing into mature, well-balanced and healthy individuals? Of course, a balance has to be struck. The caring coach has to see much further than the 'now'.

Training programmes have to look at the long-term physical, psychological, and emotional development of the individual and should take into account the following:

- basic conditioning
- the adaptation of the body to the skills being learned
- being able to apply those skills, on the mat, in grading and/or competition
- planned periods of recovery to allow the body to adapt fully to training and/or competition.

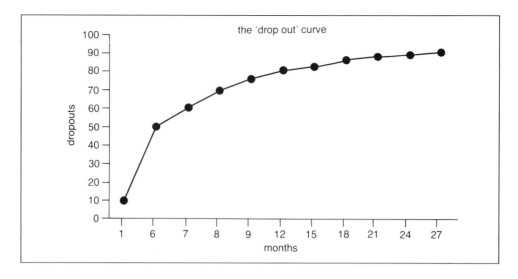

Fig. 14   Out of an initial number of 100 students, over 50 have left within 6 months of taking up martial arts. After 12 months nearly 85 have gone. The rate then slows down to the extent that after two years only 10 still train.

Training has to be carefully programmed to take all these factors into account, but the caring coach has to be aware of several other elements which have a direct effect on development. What is the genetic potential of an individual student? What is the desire of that particular student to succeed? In every case long-term development of an individual should be the most important factor.

Any long-term strategy, for example, working towards an age group championship, can be self-defeating if a child has to be overstressed to achieve what in reality is an unimportant goal. One only has to look at the drop-out rate of youngsters in the martial arts. How many who achieve early success stay in the activity, let alone maintain their elite standard? Intense specialisation too early often rebounds on both the coach and student in the search for success. This can lead to extreme frustration as the 'edge' begins to fade, leading to further frustration and disillusionment for both the coach and the student. The training load must take the following into account:

■ the amount of time available per day, week, month and year to train
■ training loads should not be too intense too early
■ general conditioning should have priority over any kind of intense specific training

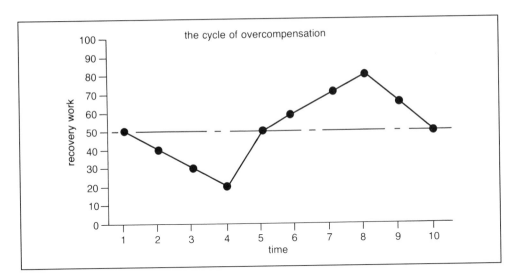

Fig. 15   The effect of training is to deplete energy reserves and produce waste products. In the recovery phase the energy reserves are 'overfilled' and the tissues overprepared for the next bout of training. If they are not used, the body will go back to its normal state.

■ technically correct techniques should be taught and learned early on so that they become well established
■ training should be balanced so that no one element is emphasised to the exclusion of others
■ the importance of recovery cannot be stressed too much; it is the recovery period which allows the body to adapt fully to training (see figs 15, 16 and 17)
■ the learning and teaching atmosphere has to be positive to allow for the student to develop at the best possible rate (see figs 18, 19 and 20).

Specialisation

It is generally accepted that a continuous and progressive programme of physical activity has many positive features, but any concerned instructor or parent has to question the increasing trend towards specialisation of coaching and training in competitive sport. The main difficulty for those involved is to identify at what age an individual is able to withstand the pressures of intensive training in its various forms.

As early as the age of 6 a child should be capable of learning and practising specific techniques and skills, although it does not follow that they will be

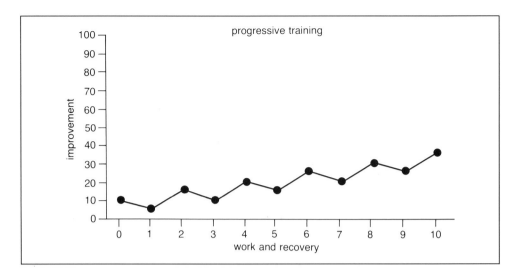

Fig. 16   If training is timed so that the next training session coincides with the overfilling of energy reserves, then the long-term effect of training will be to improve performance in a step-like fashion . . .

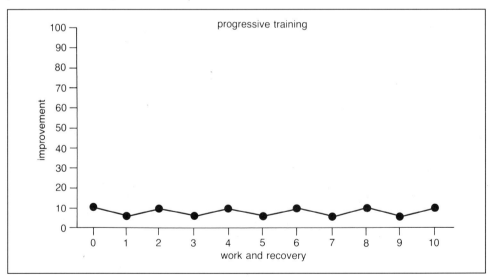

Fig. 17   . . . However, if the period of rest between sessions is too long, the benefit of the overshoot will be lost and the general level of performance will remain the same.

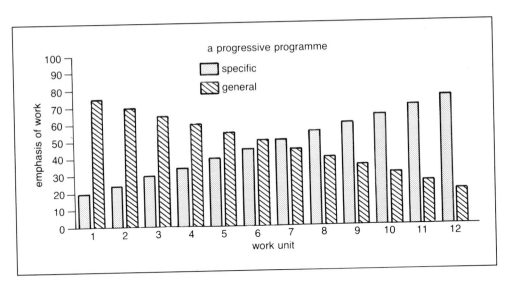

Fig. 18 In any programme of work, for example a 12-week block between gradings, there has to be a change in emphasis from the general to the specific as the work progresses.

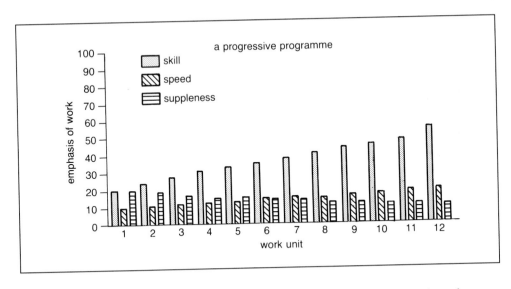

Figs 19 and 20 show how the emphasis on the individual 'S' factors changes through the 12-week programme.

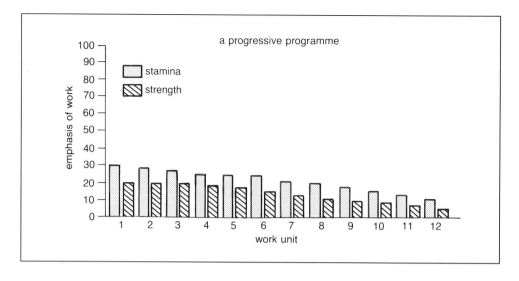

Figs 19 and 20 show how the emphasis on the individual 'S' factors changes through the 12-week programme.

either accurate or effective. How can the apparent technique of a six-year-old be as efficient as that of a fully mature individual? In all truth it cannot. A certain level of 'mimicry' is not necessarily a good thing, mainly because students do not have the intellectual development to relate, for example, the correct defence or block to an attack. This comes with maturity and experience. Most youngsters do not understand or appreciate the concept or importance of a movement or response until somewhere between the ages of 12–14 years.

It is not only the physical and intellectual maturity of the student that can lead to potential difficulties. The very activity itself can place an undesirable loading on the individual. In sports such as gymnastics, the splits and 'crab' type actions can overload the pubic symphysis and the lower spine respectively. In swimming the shoulder rotator group of muscles in all strokes can be equally susceptible to an intensive programme. Many martial arts techniques and training routines are very similar to these activities. Hip and back mobility exercises, as well as intensive shoulder work, can produce the same effect.

An intensive programme of anaerobic and aerobic activity should be delayed until at least after puberty to allow for all the hormonally controlled elements to be fully developed. With females, if started around the pubertal period, too much emphasis on endurance-type activities, which may result in weight loss, can delay the start of menstruation and the accompanying hormonal changes

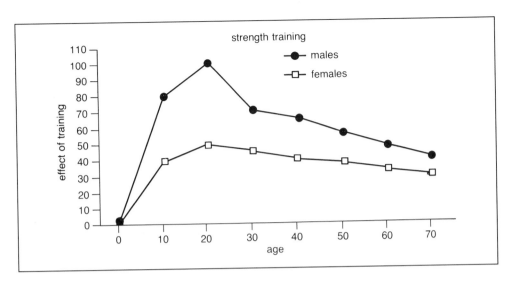

Fig. 21   Because of the major hormonal influences at puberty, the way males and females respond to strength training is very different.

by at least two years. To utilise fully the effects of any training programme androgens, or those hormones involved in building body tissue, need to be present and that will really only happen after puberty (see fig. 21).

Some youngsters are involved in activities which have weight categories. Where an intentional effort is made to keep weight down, it should be appreciated that this will coincide with the most important time in life for growth. Any conscious attempt to restrict the intake of the right nutrients in the correct amounts could have a catastrophic effect on future physical and intellectual development.

Those starting sport as early as 3 or 5 can develop a great range of mobility in a joint due to the very elastic nature of ligaments, muscle and connective tissues. However, it is difficult to say exactly when mobility training should begin. Ligaments thicken with maturity, especially over the age of 16 years. Although 'thick' ligaments are less likely to 'stretch' than immature ones, they may become inflamed or damaged if over-extended through rigorous training. At this time, more than at any other, the spine is potentially the weakest link in the interaction of body parts and therefore needs the utmost care taken with it. Within the 14 to 18 year age groupings it has to be remembered that the development of muscle mass and its associated strength can happen before the maturation of the skeleton.

Similarly, and this fact is especially important to those in the martial arts, youngsters between the ages of 5 and 11 have a low body mass and, because of their lack of musculature, a low velocity. This tends to reduce the number of contact and impact injuries!

Between the ages of 12 and 14 the massive muscle growth can overload the associated connective tissues and, in turn, the loadings on the skeletal system through training can be excessive. Because of the difficulty in predicting puberty it is essential that maturation, *not* age, be the guide during this period. Age categories for competition, for example, can be a complete nonsense. A precocious student going through puberty earlier than a student of the same chronological age will have a totally unassailable and, it has to be said, a very unfair advantage. There is some evidence to support the notion that intensive training might hasten the onset of puberty and thus might bring some advantages at the time. However, the saying 'As ye sow, so shall ye reap' should be remembered: the long-term maturational implications of such loadings should concern even the most unscrupulous adult.

It is probably fair to assert that with this age group, more than with any other, students are very aware of the television, video, film, newspaper and peer group images of the martial arts. They all want to be little Bruce Lees and Rambos! The influence of the 'ideal' or 'heroic' model assumes a tremendous importance. More often than not, it is the 'flashiness', not the skill, which catches the eye. The example might be a poor one to copy.

FITNESS TRAINING FOR THE JUNIOR MARTIAL ARTS STUDENT

'S' factors

How fit does a student need to be to participate in the martial arts? Are there different levels of fitness for different levels of ability? Is there a difference in fitness between the competitive and non-competitive martial artist?

As previously identified, the various martial arts and styles have their own particular fitness requirements. However, there are elements common to all. Fitness can be classified into the 'S' factors:

- speed
- strength
- suppleness
- stamina
- skill
- 'p'sychology.

Every martial art will have a specific 'mix' of these elements (see fig. 22).

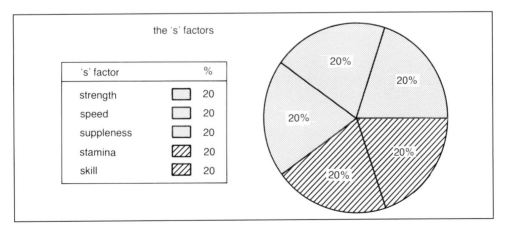

Fig. 22   It is difficult to identify the contribution of 'p'sychology in training, but the contribution of the others can and must be identified.

43

For example, some arts require a fair degree of flexibility, whereas others depend more on strength, and so on. However, all will involve each element to a certain extent. There is a great deal of medical evidence now available which suggests that any training for youngsters should be aimed at general conditioning so that all parts of the body are equally affected by exercise. Any specific training which isolates a particular limb, joint or 'S' factor must be undertaken very carefully to ensure that loads are not excessive. Certainly, until after puberty, any such training must be undertaken sparingly. Specific training for sport is dependent on physical and emotional maturity and so should only be practised by mature students.

A controversial suggestion is that we should not mould young students for the martial arts, but that we should restructure, redesign, modify and adapt the martial arts to suit the abilities of the students! Not only would this ensure a lower incidence of injuries, but it would undoubtedly lead to more students taking up the activity and staying in it for longer.

Development of the 'S' factors

Speed

Speed can be split into two main elements:

- individual limb speed, such as a punch, a kick or a block
- whole body speed (perhaps 'agility' might be a better term), such as a technique requiring the whole body to move at speed.

Youngsters do not possess the type of muscle required for fast movements; this only appears after puberty. Furthermore, any fast movements, particularly where joints are locked out with force, can cause structural damage to the soft bones. It has to be understood that speed is a refinement of technique. If a technique cannot be performed technically accurately at low or moderate speed, any attempt to practise it at high speed could result in injury, since limbs, joints and muscles are being used in the wrong movement pattern.

There is another dimension to speed which is often forgotten or misunderstood. It is usually referred to as 'reaction time'. This is a complex concept and is, in fact, made up of several inter-related elements.

- *Perception time* This means how long it takes to be aware that something is happening. Assessment is usually by visual means, but sound and touch are just as important in detecting that something is taking place.
- *Processing time* This means how long it takes to identify the type of

movement. For example, with a punch or kick, the direction and speed of the blow would be worked out during processing time.

■ *Selection time* This means how long it takes to select the correct defence or counter to an attack.
■ *Movement time* This means how long it takes to perform a selected movement.

Obviously each one of these elements takes up only a fraction of a second, but together they form the total reaction time. Any breakdown in one or more of them will affect the whole movement. Assessment will improve with practice and experience. A young student will often react quickly, but because he lacks experience he misinterprets a movement and follows on with the wrong technique. This process can only develop over a long period of time.

Strength

Strength is a very complicated notion and initially can be broken down into four types.

■ *Isotonic* The main muscle group shortens fully in the action. For example, the press-up causes the muscles, the triceps, at the back of the upper arm to shorten fully as the arms are straightened. This type of activity usually calls for a joint to be worked through its whole range of movement. It is sometimes known as 'dynamic' strength.
■ *Isometric* The main muscle group involved does not shorten. For example, the postural muscles of the trunk which are involved in maintaining a standing position do not contract fully but are in a constant state of tension. It is sometimes known as 'static' strength.
■ *Isokinetic* The main muscle group works maximally through the entire range of movement. This is normally a slower type of action and is almost a combination of isotonic and isometric strength, since there is a slow shortening of the muscle throughout the entire range. There are some movements, particularly in 'strength' katas, that are slow and controlled, and for which maximum muscular tension is held throughout the entire action.
■ *Plyometric* This is explosive strength. The maximum force of a muscle is generated in the shortest time possible. It is perhaps the type of activity which is regarded as power.

The difficulty with strengthening activities is that they do have a positive stimulating effect not only on muscle but on joints, ligaments and tendons as well, making them stronger. The skill is not to overload them. Generally

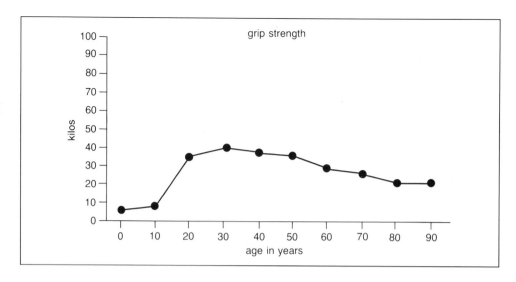

Fig. 23   For both sexes there is a rapid improvement in strength levels which peaks around 30 and only starts to decline markedly after 50.

speaking, a balanced strengthening programme will be beneficial, but a bias to one type or another could pose problems. Particular care should be taken with plyometric activities, since they create severe loadings on joints and muscles. Too much isometric or isokinetic activity can cause problems, too, in a similar fashion. It is thought beneficial to work a joint isotonically through its entire range of movement.

The picture is made even more cloudy when the load used is analysed. My rule of thumb is that weight training is inappropriate for the young martial artist. Since heavy weights can damage joints, the need for the development of maximum strength is not necessary. Strength endurance, i.e. the ability to perform a task several times, is probably the ideal type of work. Such activities, which come under the heading of 'circuit training', using body weight as a resistance to work against are those which I would recommend (if they have to be used at all) (see fig. 23).

Suppleness

Youngsters are naturally very flexible, due to the 'plastic' nature of parts of their bodies. The range of movement at a joint is governed by:

- *the type of joint* i.e.
  ball and socket, e.g. the shoulder and the hip, or

hinge, e.g. the knee and the elbow, or
sliding, e.g. the spine, the feet and the hands.
The bony structure of the joint limits movement. If the joint is taken to its limit, the bones can be damaged and tissue can float about, causing all kinds of problems.

■ *the joint capsule*
Around the joint is a sac which contains fluid to lubricate the joint. The thickness and elasticity of the sac can affect mobility. Excessive movement can inflame the sac or, at worst, tear it.

■ *ligaments*
Ligaments support the joint by keeping the bones in alignment. Often these are stretched, which can cause the bones to move out of alignment and result in damage: the joint becomes unstable.

■ *tendons*
These attach muscle to bone and are not designed to stretch. Trying to lengthen a tendon can cause damage either to the muscle or to the bone to which it is attached.

■ *skin*
The elasticity of skin decreases with age.

■ *muscle*
Muscle is made up of fibres which have to slide over each other; there is resistance to them doing so. The more muscle, the greater the resistance (see fig. 24).

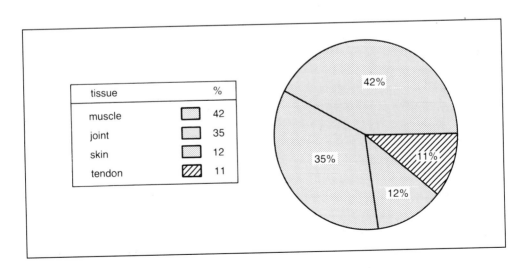

tissue		%
muscle	☐	42
joint	☐	35
skin	☐	12
tendon	▨	11

Fig. 24   Factors affecting mobility.

There is some evidence to suggest that mobility starts to decrease from the age of 8 years, and certainly from the age of 15 years. But as we have seen too much emphasis on mobility can cause structural damage. Although being very flexible may make a technique look very spectacular, it often does not make it any more effective. In fact, injuries can occur when a student tries to apply force in a range that a joint was not designed to work in.

The important element to note is that children are naturally flexible; any mobility work must be designed to maintain that degree of flexibility. Furthermore, training for mobility should go hand in hand with strengthening work to ensure that the muscles around the joints keep them stable.

Stamina

Children can cope best with aerobic activity, because they are equipped with endurance-type muscles. They are more suited to periods of low intensity work. When they are required to work at high levels of intensity they will tire very quickly. The coach must be aware that rest periods or parts of the lesson which are not physically demanding must be interspersed with activity. The student must be able to keep to the pace of the lesson; the periods of intensity and the duration of training must be carefully monitored.

The general demands of an hour's training are not the same as the specific demands of a two- or three-minute 'flat out' competition or grading. These require special preparation and it has to be stressed again that such intense periods of activity, known as anaerobic work, are not what children's bodies are best suited for. If they were anaerobic animals, the World 1500 m record would be held by a child (see fig. 25)!

However, by and large training sessions themselves will develop those aspects of aerobic and anaerobic fitness which are specific to a particular martial art. It is quite true that the best training for any martial art is to practise that martial art! At this stage in their development, because of their very active lifestyle in martial arts, at school, at play and at home, children are naturally developing these fitness characteristics. There is no need for extra sessions in either aerobic or anaerobic training.

Skill

Though children learn skills quickly, very few possess that excellence of performance which the technical manuals illustrate and top coaches would accept. They have not developed the physique to achieve perfection. Often youngsters seem like caricatures of adults, emphasising a series of non-essential elements and exaggerating others. Because they have a short attention span, they find it difficult to keep repeating a technique and to refine it. Perhaps at

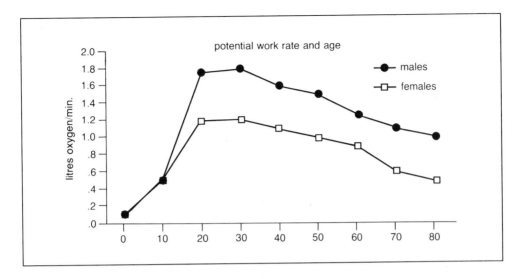

Fig. 25   As previously identified, after puberty the potential work rate of a male student improves dramatically. This is predominantly because of hormonal differences between males and females.

the very least a 'working' model of a technique which is basically sound has to be accepted. This will be refined in time. Alternatively, a series of techniques appropriate for youngsters may be introduced to serve as a foundation for technically advanced skills later on.

'P'sychology

Whatever reason youngsters have for taking up a martial art, it is essential that students are given the best environment in which to learn. Children learn a great deal by copying, so it is important that the model they are imitating is not only technically accurate but has the right personal standards of behaviour and conduct. This element of good coaching is identified in the M.A.C. Coach Education Programme. It cannot be stressed too much that values and skills learned during this period of physical and mental development will influence children's performance in and out of the dojo for the rest of their lives.

It is my belief that the coach of the young martial artist has a major role to play in the short-term development of the individual and in the long-term development of the sport. It is vital that instructors blend very carefully the 'S' factors in their lessons to achieve results. They will ensure not only the correct physical, mental, technical and personal development of individuals, but also more effective, efficient and safe coaches for the future.

TRAINING REQUIREMENTS

When we talk about training for the martial arts there is an obvious problem in that each one has its specific fitness requirements. So, it may be helpful to look at the differences in preparation for the more popular arts.

Karate

Karate is probably the most popular martial art with youngsters in terms of the total number of students training. However, the problem with karate is that it is based on impact-type activities, such as kicks and punches. Physically immature students may inadvertently damage hands and feet from impact on hard surfaces, so their training should be carefully monitored. Any attempt to 'harden' the feet and the hands using makiwara or special exercises, such as finger tip and knuckle press ups, should not be undertaken. Similarly, in sparring activities protective pads must be worn to prevent damage from impact. Full contact and breaking techniques have no place in the training of junior martial artists.

The traditional style of karate, and most other martial arts, requires the students to train in class lines. This poses no problems where the aim is to develop both technique and excellence of movement. However, care must be taken not to lock out the arms and knees at speed, as this puts tremendous loadings on the joints. The use of katas is probably one of the best training methods for karate, for in their sequences are developed techniques, blocks and counter-attacks in a controlled and safe fashion.

Basically, the type of training in a lesson is aerobic, since a student can be active for over an hour. However, there are going to be periods of intense physical activity in which the work will be predominantly anaerobic. The coach should bear in mind that the young martial artist does not have the physical maturity to deal with this type of work. Not only is he unable to work as intensively as the older students, but he also cannot continue for as long. The implication for the lesson is brief periods of maximum effort should be interspersed with long periods of rest. Students should not be totally inactive during these rest periods, but should perhaps perform kata-type activities.

Karate relies predominantly on explosive, powerful action in both the legs and arms. With the physically immature martial artist, both the action and the loadings on muscles, tendons, ligaments, bones and joints are particularly dangerous. The teaching emphasis must be on the learning of correct technique, rather than on its use. Technique will come with maturation as strength, speed, and power develop with skeletal growth.

Jiu jitsu

Jiu jitsu was historically a highly effective martial art from which has developed many current styles, particularly the Olympic sport of judo. The emphasis on impact is much less than in karate, the aim being to throw an opponent off guard rather than cause damage. Though punching and kicking are an important aspect of technique, the emphasis is on blocking and locking skills. The essence is defence and restraint, rather than offence.

Jiu jitsu tends to be a flowing series of techniques where the emphasis is on control rather than on impact. Of course, for the young martial artist this means that there will be no overloading the immature body systems; the main aim is to apply technique and not to use force.

Again, the introduction of katas is very helpful for the young student. Impact injuries are less of a problem than in karate, but care must be taken when applying locks. Immature, and therefore easily damaged, joints are especially vulnerable.

Like karate, some skills are taught to students in lines, but in this case they are usually in pairs. Novices take it in turn to practise the application of techniques. Generally, the work load is aerobic, but occasionally very intensive activity is called for which the coach should be aware of in terms of overall lesson planning. The main difference between karate and jiu jitsu is in the emphasis of speed. Karate tends to isolate limb speed, and concentrates on the fast kick or punch, Jiu jitsu tends to emphasise whole body speed or agility which reduces the loadings on the young martial artist.

Judo

Judo as both an 'art' and a 'sport' tends to place its emphasis firstly on a grappling-type activity through which the attacker can find an advantage to trip, throw, lock or hold down an opponent. Although at the highest levels judo is intensive and demanding, particularly in competition, it need not be so for the young martial artist. Normally practice is in pairs, with the students taking it in turns to apply a technique. Since there is no punching or kicking, the danger to the student is less than in, for example, karate, but the use of locks has to be carefully monitored. Under no circumstances should any choking holds be allowed. In 'traditional' judo there were many katas which are not taught today. These could be an invaluable part of the lesson for youngsters.

It is essential, because of the number of throwing techniques employed, that breakfalls in their varied fashion are fully covered. Falling backwards, sideways and forwards in an ineffective manner can overload very vulnerable parts of the body. This must not be allowed to happen.

Aikido

Traditionally aikido involves little in the way of explosive action, though this cannot be said of the sport! Like jiu jitsu, whole body speed, or agility, is more important than limb speed. Aikido tends to concentrate on using the opponent's force, that is it is not offensive, but is defensive in nature.

The emphasis tends to be on the use of a series of flowing techniques which depend on skill rather than on effort. The main thrust of aikido seems to be on the psychological, as opposed to the physical; it is a form of martial arts 'chess'! Such emphasis could be borne in mind by practitioners of other martial arts. Training usually involves two students taking turns to apply techniques; this should allow for a recovery between periods of semi-intensive activity.

Hapkido

Hapkido typically is a combination of the punches and kicks from karate and the flowing grappling and throwing skills from aikido. The emphasis tends to be on the execution of good and appropriate technique, rather than on brute force. However, the possible dangers of impact techniques and of applied locks and blocks should not be forgotten.

Again, the teaching styles of hapkido are very similar to those of karate and jiu jitsu; students are in rank and file, and are taught kata and partner work.

Kendo

Though kendo is an impact-based activity, using the bamboo sword known as a shinai, the dangers are somewhat reduced by a full set of body and head armour. The loading on immature bodies is very much limited, the main thrust of the effort being in the application of technique and the correct state of mind. Training tends to be dominated by sparring, but an element of class activity and katas seems well suited to the young student.

Kung fu

For me kung fu continues to be an enigma. There are so many styles and family interpretations that it is very difficult to identify any common themes, especially when one considers the notion of 'hard' and 'soft' forms. The focus of all styles, however, seems to be on the application of inner energy or chi. Though strikes and kicks are used, the speed with which they are practised does not really pose any problems, especially in tai chi where the essential elements are relaxation and form.

The extensive use of both long and short form katas can only add to kung fu's benefits for the younger student, since immature systems are not being overloaded. The inclusion of class drills and sparring as other elements completes the lesson.

However, great care must be taken with 'innovative' training methods. The use of wooden mannequins is not to be recommended, because of the potential danger of permanent injury to joints, connective tissue and bones.

Shorinji kempo

Shorinji kempo has a very similar fitness requirement to hapkido, and training tends to follow a similar pattern. However, there is a greater emphasis on the philosophy behind the development of the style.

A psychological approach to the activity is taken, and stress is laid on the development of a correct attitude and state of mind for the application of techniques in general and of training in particular. The need for a clear mind and the development of self-reliance is nurtured.

Tang soo do

The requirements of tang soo do are very similar to those of karate, but there is perhaps greater emphasis on higher and more kicking techniques (like those in taekwando). Training tends to follow a very similar pattern to that for karate.

Taekwando

Taekwando is very similar to karate, and has a strong bias towards leg techniques. However, there is a trend for full-contact and breaking techniques, both of which must be avoided by the coach of the young martial artist. Again, training is very similar in nature to that of karate.

Thai boxing

Thai boxing has close connections with boxing and the full-contact martial arts, and so appropriate precautions need to be taken. It is perhaps surprising to learn that it also has a religious background; the associated Buddhist philosophy plays a very important role for the higher grades.

As in boxing, the emphasis is on sparring, though great use is made of punch bags and pads, shin and foot guards, and gloves. Shadow boxing, which is likely to be less hazardous than boxing proper for the young student, should have a place in training.

General considerations

It can be seen that there is some degree of uniformity in the training for most of the more popular martial arts. Lessons are traditionally between one-and-a-half and two hours in length, and tend to be divided into sections of class 'drills', partner work or sparring, and kata or form work. Generally speaking, because of the length of time involved, there is constant activity at a low level of intensity. This is exactly what the young student can cope with best. However, there may be periods of intense work, which will pose a problem since the student can manage only short bursts and needs a period of recovery afterwards. Unless performing in competition and grading, where bouts of very intense work may last two or three minutes, both fatigue and recovery have to be considered.

Partner work

Partner work is common to many of the martial arts and allows for students to alternate between being fully active and passive, hopefully recovering. Sparring, however, tends to require both students to work flat out and so special allowances must be made for periods of rest or recovery. (Furthermore, precautions will have to be taken to prevent impact or overloading injuries.) These periods of recovery could be taken up with individual practice of technique or the development of katas so that the rest between strenuous activity can be productive. Whether the current structure of training and lesson design are appropriate to the young martial artist is for the coach to decide. But in so doing he must take into account all the special requirements that the student needs for safe, appropriate and effective learning.

TRAINING INJURIES

The caring coach who has wisely structured his students' training programme should be reading this chapter for information only! Training injuries, apart from those accidents resulting in cuts and bruises, should not occur. Healthy, vigorous activity will never be completely without risk, but it is the coach's responsibility to see that training does not involve unnecessary dangers.

The coach must be vigilant at all times and should monitor the reaction of each student to training. Any problem should be identified and dealt with immediately before it develops into something more serious. It is essential that medical advice and treatment are obtained quickly, not only to resolve the current problem but to avoid any possible long-term complications.

Most injuries which young students develop are linked to the bones, joints, tendons, ligaments and associated muscle. Immature bone is soft and can easily be damaged; this is why overloading limbs and joints is not recommended. But perhaps more importantly all growth in bones occurs at the ends where they meet with other bones, i.e. at the joint (see figs 26 and 27). Any damage to these

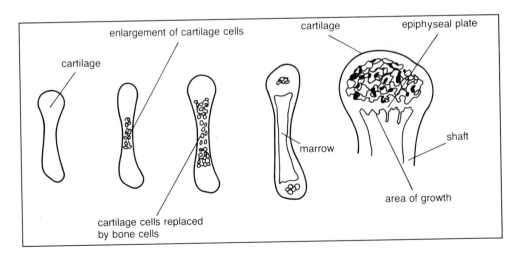

Fig. 26   The development of immature bone to mature bone, particularly the development of the 'growth areas', can be clearly seen.

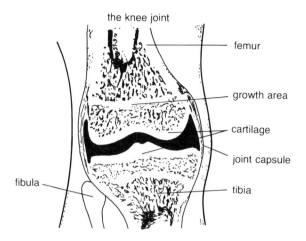

Fig. 27 A typical joint showing the main characteristics.

soft growth areas can result in no further development taking place. For example, damage to the growth areas of the hip bone could result in the leg not growing properly and so it could be considerably shorter than the other (see fig. 28). This may sound unlikely, but it does happen. This is why such practices as knuckle and finger tip press-ups should not be practised by the young student; the potential for long-term damage is very high.

Similarly, any full-contact practices should not be used until maturity has been reached. In punching or kicking activities full extension of the arm or leg must not occur either at speed or, where the limb straightens, with great force. Unloaded fast kicks or punches to the air or powerful techniques used against a pad or bag are typical problem areas because they overload the joints, especially the knees, elbows, feet and hands. This can result in damage to the structure of the joints and to the growth areas of the bones, particularly those of the feet and hands. Ideally, locks to joints should not be applied, but if they have to be they should only be done in a token fashion. The rule, therefore, must be not to subject young martial artists to extreme loadings or to continued use of one particular part of the body over a long period.

A survey of junior martial artists has revealed that over 30% had a current injury at the time they were questioned and that nearly 70% had been injured in training in the recent past. Even more worrying was the fact that when asked about the situation in general the instructors were unaware of their students' difficulties. The problem would appear to be quite widespread. There can be no room for complacency; the coach must be aware at all times of possible troubles a student may encounter.

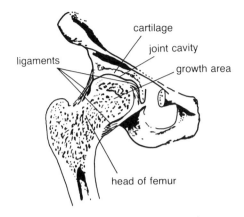

Fig. 28   The hip joint.

Knuckle press-ups should not be practised by the young martial artist

Ensure that punch pads or bags are able to absorb the impact of a kick or a punch

Types of injury

Injuries in training fall broadly into two main categories.

Momentary high stress or loading

This can be the result of:

- a bad landing, particularly from a height
- a bad fall
- a poorly performed breakfall
- a poorly performed technique
- a mistimed technique.

Overuse injuries

These occur when a student over a period of time constantly overloads a particular part of the body (see fig. 29). These tend to be:

- the shoulders, elbows, wrists and hands
- the upper spine and neck
- the lower spine
- the hips and pelvic girdle
- the hamstrings
- the knees
- the Achilles tendon
- the ankles, arches and toes.

Any sign of an injury must be noted and the student should not be allowed to work that particular part of the body until treatment and/or a full recovery have occurred and the 'all-clear' is given. There really is no excuse for an overuse injury. It shows a lack of observation and care on the part of the coach. Furthermore, like all injuries at this stage of development, the future implications cannot be foreseen. The long-term effects of any injury at an early age can continue for the rest of the student's life.

It is not possible to describe each and every injury which the young martial artist might develop, but the most common ones seem to be the following.

Acromio-clavicular joint injury

The collar bone is attached to the shoulder blade by a series of ligaments. Impact injuries to this joint from kicks, punches and bad falls can put strain on the ligaments. Inflammation and associated pain are the result. However,

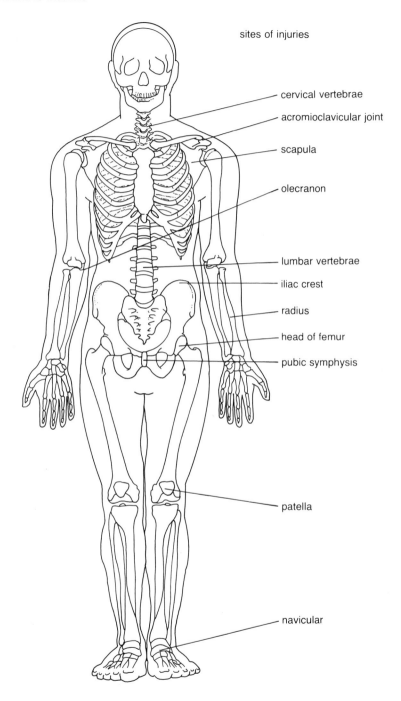

sites of injuries

cervical vertebrae

acromioclavicular joint

scapula

olecranon

lumbar vertebrae

iliac crest

radius

head of femur

pubic symphysis

patella

navicular

Fig. 29   The skeletal system, identifying the main areas of injuries.

repeated injury to the site can cause the ligaments to tear and bumps can appear on the collarbone itself.

Shoulder injuries

The shoulder joint is one of the most freely movable and equally complex joints in the body. The joint is supported by a series of muscles and tendons which ensure not only the correct pattern of movement but its stability as well. Overuse of the joint will lead to inflammation of the tendon attachments of the muscles, causing further inflammation and pain.

A resistance to certain ranges of movement is often associated with this condition as swollen tissue is restricted from its normal movement within the joint. With bad falls or poor technique it is possible to tear muscle or its tendons. In some cases overuse of the joint can lead to calcium nodules being formed which can cause even more inflammation and damage to the tissue close to them.

Olecranon bursitis

At the tip of the elbow is a small bursa, a fluid-filled sac. A fall or blow to this can cause damage leading to inflammation, swelling and pain.

Javelin elbow

Though the javelin has not been identified as a 'traditional' martial arts weapon, there are similarities between the injuries which athletes and martial artists experience. The muscles in the forearm which control the position of the wrist in every technique are attached to the upper arm bone at the elbow. Javelin elbow produces tenderness and pain just above the elbow joint. Overuse of rotational movements, particularly with weapons for which a poor grip is used, can exacerbate the problem. Gripping and twisting techniques may also cause difficulties.

Radial fractures

Where the bones of the forearm (the radius and the ulna) meet at the elbow joint there is the possibility of damage. Because of the soft nature of the bone a heavy fall onto a straight arm, a violent punch against solid resistance or overuse can cause the head of the radius to degenerate or the bone to break. As a result of the damaged bone and particles which might be floating about in the joint, there is often difficulty in straightening the arm and pain is felt on the outer side of the elbow.

This activity, sometimes called 'the stubborn donkey', places great stress on the muscles and vertebrae of the neck. Any similar activities will have the same effect

Spinal injuries

There are few techniques which use the spine directly, but any action will require force to be transmitted from one part of the body to the other, that is, via the spine. Similarly, any whole body action or agility will require not only stability but mobility of the spine. It is the need for the spine both to bear loads and to be flexible that causes most of the problems.

Neck injuries

The neck is a very vulnerable area of the spine and great care must be taken in any forward, backward, sideways or rotational activity. A blow to the head can also be a cause for concern if the bones of the neck are damaged in the process. Injuries to these areas can range from damage at the joint between two vertebrae, which might involve the discs that separate them or the joint capsule, to structural damage to the bones themselves. Connective tissue which supports the spine, that is, tendons, ligaments and the muscles of the back, are also vulnerable. Tissue can become swollen and inflamed which produces pain. Obviously major structural damage potentially has very serious consequences.

Lower back injuries

The same problems which occur with the neck can affect the lower back. There are two activities in particular which must be practised with care. Arching the back in a backward movement, i.e. in 'crab' fashion, can affect all of the elements of the spine and it can also lead to damage of the vertebrae if taken to extremes. This in turn can cause inflammation and pain and, if there is much damage, permanent discomfort and restricted movement. The joint between the spine and the pelvis is very vulnerable, too, and so care must be taken to keep the joint aligned during activity. For example, during sit-up exercises legs should not be straight since it places an undue strain on the joint. Much lower back pain and soreness can be traced to this bad practice.

The photograph overleaf shows a very common exercise used in martial arts. This really is not a good activity because of the loading on the lower spine. If the back is to be strengthened it is far better that correct lifting technique is emphasised with the use of a medicine ball.

Good lifting technique

Overloading the upper and lower spine is a problem with this sort of practice

Perthe's disease

The hip joint can pose problems, particularly with the ball head of the thigh bone. With sudden impacts, such as landings, and/or kicks the head of the bone can become damaged. Since this is the growth area of the bone, any damage can have major consequences. Growth of the bone can be affected: it may slow down or even stop.

Iliac crest epiphysitis

The top of the pelvis is important for growth. Techniques that involve violent twisting and/or constant turning, which uses the attached muscles of the abdomen and lower back, can lead to damage. There can be inflammation with overuse and a degree of pain.

Osteitis pubis

The pelvis is made up of two dish-shaped bones which meet at the pubic symphysis just above the genitalia. Splits which involve moving the legs apart, forwards and backwards and to the side, are a particular problem. High kicks and kicks requiring the leg to be raised away from the body to the side can also aggravate the condition. Constant practice will lead to inflammation and pain at the site of the symphysis.

Osgood Schlatter's disease

Just below the kneecap (the patella) there is a ligament which attaches it to the top of the shin bone. Kicking, low squats, too many poor landings from techniques which require a high jump and, more importantly, a soft landing can aggravate the condition. There is tenderness to the touch, as well as pain and possible localised swelling which is associated with the top of the shin bone just below the knee. Kneeling or extending the leg with force will generally cause discomfort and in some cases considerable pain.

Squatter's or jumper's knee

Similar in its location to Osgood Schlatter's disease, this problem is associated more with inflammation of the patellar ligament. The problem is generally found in students who practise activities requiring a bent knee, for example, landings from a high jump and slowing down too quickly from shuttle runs.

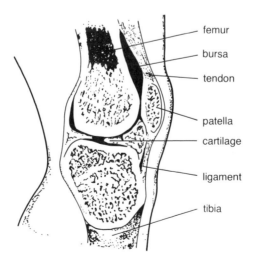

Fig. 30   The knee joint

Sever's disease

This occurs at the point where the Achilles tendon is attached to the heel, and may result from prolonged jumping and running activities. It can produce inflammation and pain. Continued overuse can lead to further swelling and associated pain.

Plantar fasciitis

The arch of the foot is maintained by a strong band of connective tissue called the plantar fascia. In techniques which require a vigorous take-off, especially from a hard surface, the plantar fascia is stretched. Inflammation and pain can develop at the points where it is attached to the bone, particularly under the front part of the heel and in the arch of the foot.

Navicular osteochondritis

Many martial arts include jumping techniques. Naturally, great forces have to be absorbed on landing, and the feet obviously bear most of the brunt. Just in front of and below the ankle is a bone called the navicular which absorbs a great amount of force from the toes and arch. Overloading can cause inflammation and swelling, with associated pain. In severe cases the bone can degenerate, in which case range of movement may be seriously affected.

There are several general conditions that can occur in any part of the body which may affect the young student. These are as follows.

Bursitis

Sacs of fluid, bursae, surround most joints and many tendons in the body, lubricating tissues which tend to move against each other. A sudden impact or constant overuse can cause damage, inflammation, swellings and associated pain.

Tendonitis

All muscles are attached to bone by tendons. Constant strain on these tendons can result in inflammation and possible swelling, with a fair amount of pain and discomfort when the affected tendons and muscles are used (see fig. 31).

Tenosynovitis

Many tendons are encapsulated by bursae. Any damage to the sac can lead to inflammation and pain due to the swelling of tissue and a loss in the free movement of the tendon.

section through a muscle

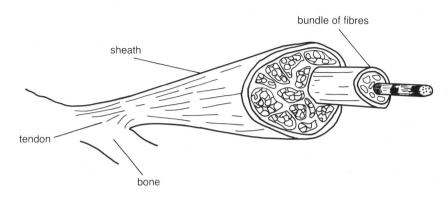

Fig. 31   A typical skeletal muscle and tendon attachment.

Osteochondritis

This condition is readily identified as a problem with youngsters. How many of us have heard of the problem of 'growing pains'? Osteochondritis occurs when the growing areas of the bones are overused or are subject to intensive use and so become inflamed. As we have seen, continued use in such a situation could cause permanent damage. Care must be taken to ensure that this condition does not arise.

Asthma

There is another condition that affects the young martial artist which one cannot really describe as being directly 'structural'. There is a growing awareness in the medical and sport science world of the seemingly ever increasing presence of asthma. As most people know, asthma manifests itself as an extreme shortage of breath which can be very distressing to the individual concerned and to onlookers alike.

Basically, asthma is either brought on through stress or it is linked to an allergy. Obviously the caring coach can reduce the amount of physical or psychological stress which an individual is subjected to and can also be sensitive enough to ensure that any medication, such as an inhaler, is readily available should an attack occur.

Weight categories

Apart from the obvious age categories in the competitive martial arts, there are also weight categories to consider. While youngsters are growing, it is essential that they eat the right type of food in the correct amounts. Any reduction in food intake to make a particular weight class could have unforeseen and devastating long-term effects on general health. This can be seen especially with girls. They should at all times ensure a percentage body fat of *at least 12%*. Should they fall below this level during weight-limiting diets, not only will their periods be delayed (or stopped altogether) but the regulation of bone development will be markedly affected. Insufficient calcium will be laid down as bone; very early on in life this may result in poor growth patterns and later on it might lead to osteoporosis or a rapid degeneration of the skeleton.

THE LEARNING ENVIRONMENT

It is essential that the training session is designed to teach skills in the most efficient and effective manner. Without dwelling too long on the pedagogical aspects of lesson planning the following guidelines might be of help.

Be methodical

Develop a regular routine of lesson planning:

- introduction
- introductory activities, including the warm-up
- review of last session's skills
- new skills
- class activity
- group activity
- pairs' practice
- concluding activities, including the warm-down.

Be visible

Nearly 75% of the learning process takes place through watching skills and techniques; in other words, instructors are examples to copy. Traditional rank and file student organisation tends to mean that not everyone, especially those at the back, can see the teacher and/or the demonstration properly. It is essential, therefore, that when demonstrating a technique, especially a new one, all students should have a clear view.

Be audible

With a large group it is essential that the teacher is able to project his voice so that everyone can hear clearly. Nearly 15% of the learning process involves being given a verbal description of what is required. This can be even more effective when used at the same time as a demonstration.

A variety of volume and tone in the voice will ensure the attention of all individuals. Make sure that you project your voice in an appropriate manner for the size of the group involved. Poor acoustics in the training hall will also have to be taken into account. Equally important is the choice of words. Make sure that clear and precise instructions are given.

Be concise

When providing information make sure that you are succinct and to the point and that your message is appropriate to the age and understanding of the students.

Be relevant

When using demonstrations explain in general terms what the technique is and how it might be applied in the 'real world'. Tell the students what to look for. Show them the technique from a variety of angles so that they gain a clear picture of what is involved. 'Talking through' the technique, that is identifying the essential components—preparation, action and completion—is good practice.

Be constructive with criticism

When commenting on a student's technique identify one problem at a time.

Be positive

Encourage all the time, even if improvement is only gradual. Any technique or activity will have some good features, however small. Show an interest in each and every student.

THEORY INTO PRACTICE

In the previous sections I have looked at the physical and psychological factors which have a profound effect on the training of junior martial artists. In this section I will show how all the elements which have been outlined can be applied to appropriate, systematic, progressive and safe training. My main aim is to look at the way the individual learns progressively more complex skills as he grows both in physical stature and in intellect (see fig. 32).

The activities described are designed to take the very young student with little general co-ordination or ability to a point of preparedness at which he is ready in both mind and body to begin to learn those very specific and complex techniques of the martial arts (see fig. 33).

As I pointed out earlier, it should not be assumed that when youngsters, and possibly even mature students, begin training they have developed the repertoire of basic skills of body control, agility, co-ordination and general condition that are a necessary prerequisite to future success. The activities covered here are designed to show the caring coach how he can incorporate sound educational and physiological principles into the training programme.

skill development in the martial arts

stage 1	a basic pattern of movement
stage 2	a crude attempt at the technique
stage 3	technical refinement
stage 4	adaptation
stage 5	physiological adaptation

Fig. 32   From a grasp of the basic movement pattern the stages of skill development are identified.

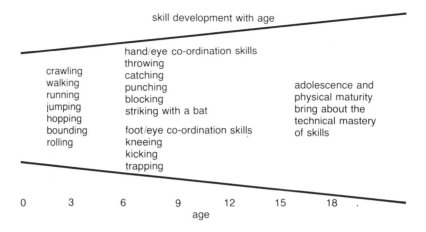

Fig. 33   The development of the skill learning process.

The various practices can be seen as separate drills and games, or as specific parts of a well-designed lesson. Their place in the programme must be left to the coach's discretion.

Fundamental skills

Going back to absolute movement patterns can be instructive and fun. There are few activities that are more basic than the *guerrilla crawl*. In this game students crawl along the dojo, keeping the whole of their forearms and shins in contact with the floor.

The *crouch walk* is a natural progression since it puts more loading on to the hands and feet.

A more strenuous version of what looks like an elementary form of movement is the *seal walk*. For this the legs are allowed to drag on the floor while the arms do all the work, moving forwards one at a time. There are many other activities which have the same benefits of developing skill and physical prowess; the coach needs to apply a little imagination in adapting such games for his class.

All of these activities can be used as introductory exercises or as part of the warm-up; they can also be used in relays. By modifying them slightly more of a fun element can be brought in. Interestingly, in the photograph below even more control than usual is demanded from the student: in order to dribble the ball under control a fair amount of concentration and co-ordination must be used. Many crawling type activities can be adapted in such a way. Again, they may serve as introductory activities, relays or even games, e.g. 'crawling football'.

The guerrilla crawl

The crouch walk

The seal walk

The crab walk, devised as part of the 'walking' theme practice

The guerrilla dribble

Posture

With a reasonable command of such basic movement the student is able to progress on to the next level of skill development. The student's posture is very important for the development of advanced techniques, so it follows that any defects are identified right from the start. Basic requirements of good posture are erect head, no round shoulders, straight back and no pronounced foot displacement. If a student cannot stand properly at the outset, how can he hope later to hold the variety of stances needed for effective technique? Through observation of students standing in class lines and by generally walking around in the lesson the coach must make some assessment of the students' posture and deportment, since both will have a marked effect on the natural progression into running activities. Whereas everyone naturally will adopt a style of walking or running which suits their own particular body shape, it still must conform to both biomechanical principles and good 'form'.

Stopping with two feet

A single-foot stop

Walking and running

Being able to walk and run in an acceptable fashion leads on to being able to stop under control. It will be difficult at a later stage, when a student has to move at speed from one technique to another, if he has not learned the basic skill of stopping one action before progressing on to the next. 'Whistle stop' activities are quite effective in developing this ability. The students walk or run in a controlled fashion around the floor area, stopping immediately under control when they hear a whistle or a shout. Various types of stop can be tried using both feet or one foot forward; or the feet can be alternated. Variations on running and walking include hopping on either leg; 'giant strides' and *hopping tag* can be included as a development.

Jumping

A basic level of co-ordination is required before the student can progress into a series of bounding activities which need control on both take-off and landing. Jumping up and down on the spot is a good way of starting and can be developed into the very useful activity of skipping. Varying the skipping technique can add variety to this much maligned and yet very valuable activity.

Skipping is an excellent practice

Jump the rope. The weighted rope is swung round at ground level for students to jump over

Excellent range of movement is shown in this straddle jump

Tuck jumps can be fun!

With the integration of running skills many different take-offs and landings can be practised. A development of this activity is to include a half- or full-turn in the air, landing with control and ready to go into the next activity.

Speed can now be generated and can be used in a controlled manner to generate height in jumping activities. With a good run-up and vigorous take-off, sufficient height can be generated to perform different types of jump, such as the straddle jump and the tucked jump.

Using equipment

With the use of very simple equipment an element of variety may be introduced and this will aid progression. Double-footed *bunny hops* from side to side and along the length of an object, e.g. a belt, can be a good start. It can be made more difficult by raising the height of the object to be jumped over. Cones can be very useful items of equipment for this activity, since they can be put in an upright or a horizontal position.

(Top left) Side-to-side bunny hops . . .

(Top right) . . . and a variation . . .

. . . and an even more difficult variation

Bunny hops in a straight line over low obstacles . . .

. . . or even over higher obstacles

Similarly, *bunny hops* in a straight line can be practised. A wide range of hopping, stepping and jumping activities over cones can now be performed with variations in speed, take-offs and landings under control and with good form.

ROLLING

Success with variations in rolling skills depends on students having a fair understanding of where the various parts of their body are, which direction they are travelling in and at what speed. If students are ultimately going to have to learn a series of breakfalls, and falls of a more uncontrolled nature, they need to have a sound grounding in elementary rolling activities (see fig. 34).

Possibly the simplest of all these activities is the *kipper roll*. Here the student starts the activity lying on his stomach. He can roll to his right on to his back and, continuing the turn, on to his stomach once again. He can move either to the left or to the right.

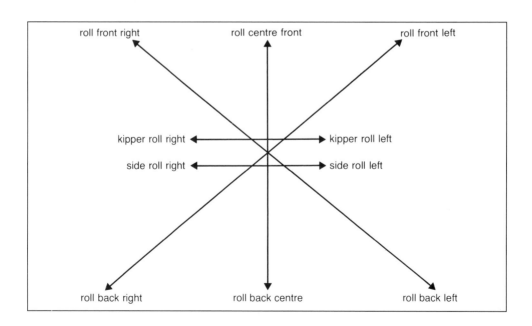

Fig. 34   The rolling 'directional cross'.

(Above) The kipper roll starting position

(Below) The mid-way point

Completion of the kipper roll

The starting position for the side roll

A progression from the *kipper roll* is the *side roll*. In the example shown, the student kneels on his left knee, and his right leg is straight out to the side. The movement begins with the left shoulder being pushed down to the floor and across his body to the right side. This will cause the student to roll on his back from his left shoulder to the right. Keeping the movement going, he will come upright on to his right knee, followed by the left leg which straightens. Obviously students can roll to the right or to the left.

The mid-way point

Completion of the side roll

A good, tight tucked position for the start of the right diagonal roll

Most students will find little difficulty with either of these rolls. However, the classical forward and backward rolls can cause problems. Being upside down, which is a requirement of both activities, and trying to position the head out of the way can be worrying. Anxiety will naturally affect the quality and efficiency of the movement.

When introducing forward or backward movements there is a tendency for students not to get their head to the floor but to roll over the right or left shoulder. This can, in fact, be used to advantage. At the start of a right front *diagonal roll* the student drops the right forearm to the floor and then proceeds

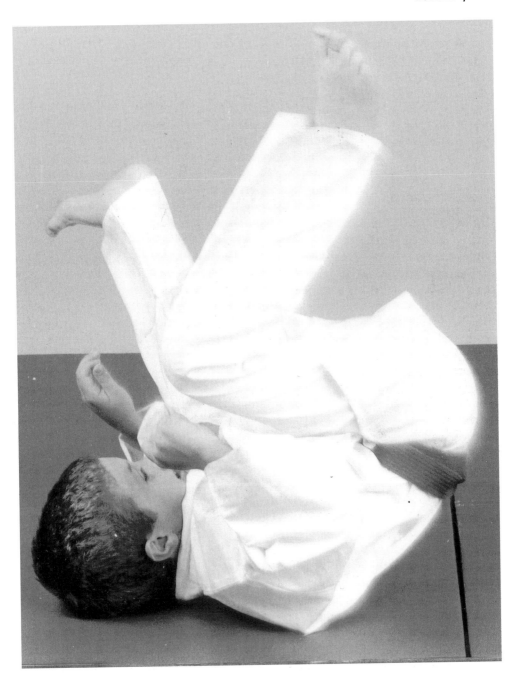

Keeping the tight tuck

The starting position of the forward roll

Completion of the roll

*Keeping the tuck and getting the hands down
on to the floor*

to roll over the right shoulder, keeping the movement to the right and coming back into the crouch position. In such an action the student really pivots over he shoulder, keeping the head safely out of the way. It is also possible to roll diagonally front left and, just as easily, to roll diagonally back right and left.

The *forward roll* depends upon the student being able to tuck his chin into his chest in the first part of the movement. Hands should be kept in contact with the floor for as long as possible to keep body weight off the head. The roll is completed when the student overbalances forwards to come up into a crouch position.

Finishing position for the forward roll

The *backward roll* requires a similar action. From a crouch position, with the chin tucked firmly into the chest the student overbalances backwards, aiming to get his hands down fast to support his weight as he rolls over his head. He finishes in a crouch position. (See photographs overleaf.)

Once the student has mastered various rolls they can be put together into a *rolling kata*. Further development can be made by starting rolls from a half squat and then from a standing position. As a final development, once the basic skill has been fully learned, dive rolls over barriers of increasing height can be practised. A note of caution: if rolls are to be practised for height or at speed the appropriate crash mats must be used in the interest of safety.

The backward roll starting position

Finishing position

The hands go down quickly to take the weight

COMBAT GAMES

Up to now little has been said about direct competition or partner work. One of the essential aspects of the martial arts is that competition, grading and training require the students to work together in either a spirit of conflict or co-operation. This type of relationship can only be developed through activities which mirror the required characteristic. Students will not be able to work together and sustain the pressures of the competitive situation or the training environment at a high level if they have not learned how to do so at a lower level.

It is important to realise that the combat games described here naturally follow on from the previous running, jumping and rolling activities. Experience of rolling will be particularly valuable, since in some of the 'rough and tumble' students may unintentionally end up on the floor and so may need to utilise their rolling skills.

Examples of games

Arm wrestling is probably one of the most basic direct combat activities. But here again, as the students develop co-ordination, with a little imagination the practice can be modified to become more demanding. For example, students

Arm wrestling

Arm wrestling in a kneeling position

Single-handed tug-of-war

Arm wrestling in a standing position

can use their left as well as their right arms. The activity tends to be rather static in that there is no general body movement, but this can be quickly rectified.

Elbow wrestling, which involves interlocking the elbows, adds the extra dimension of pulling. In the illustration the right arms are being used; the left arms should not, of course, be neglected.

(Right) Elbow wrestling

Through-the-legs tug-of-war

Crossed-arm tug-of-war

A variation on the wrestling theme is *single-handed tug-of-war*. The combatants stand toe to toe and try to pull each other off balance. In *through-the-legs tug-of-war* the students stand back to back, reach through their legs to take hold of their opponents' hands and try to pull them in their direction. In *crossed-arm tug-of-war* the students face each other, with their arms crossed, and try to pull their opponent in their direction.

Pushing-type activities can be practised in a similar way. For *bouncing tops* the students keep low, bouncing on the balls of their feet, and try to push each other over using only the palms of their hands on the palms of their opponents. The game can be altered slightly so that students keep their arms folded.

In *hopping tops* the students are only allowed to move by hopping and they try to push their opponents back by using their folded arms.

In *bent-over straight-arm push* students put their hands on their opponents' shoulders and, keeping both arms straight, try to push each other backwards. During the game of *shoulder push* the students put their right shoulders against each other and push!

(Left) Bouncing tops (Right) Bent-over straight-arm push

Hopping tops

Shoulder push

Free for all

A further development of these pushing and pulling activities involves an element of team work and/or co-operation with others. For example, in *free for all* each student tries to pull in his own direction. Knotted belts or a rope can be very useful.

In *team tug-of-war* there are equally balanced sides, the number being related to the length of the rope or belt. In a variation, belts and ropes are dispensed with. During *line tug-of-war* students pull backwards, or face forwards and pull in a sideways movement. The line can be of any length.

Team tug-of-war

Team tug-of-war without a 'rope'!

Backwards tug-of-war

Forwards tug-of-war

USING EQUIPMENT

Up to now the student has only has to handle his body in a controlled fashion during a variety of increasingly demanding situations. It is probably the right point in the development of skill acquisition to introduce a simple piece of equipment, a sponge ball!

Gentle two-handed throwing and catching can be practised with a partner. The ability to judge distance, speed and effort is developed by these simple actions. Progression involves throwing and catching with either the right or left hand, and using different angles of arm movement, for example, in a sitting-down position.

Crouch catching requires the students to maintain a crouch position while throwing and catching the ball first with two hands and then, as the skill develops, with only one.

Throwing a ball with both hands   *Catching with both hands*

Sitting down and trying to catch a ball with only one hand
Catching with one hand

Throwing and catching from a crouching position

Free fall throw-and-catch

Free fall can be a strenuous way to develop skills. Keeping legs, knees and feet as far off the ground as possible the students have to throw and catch, with their arms and shoulders held as high as possible. Using two hands is difficult; using only one can be nearly impossible!

Strange variations can be invented by the coach, such as *through-the-legs throwing*. The student throws the ball backwards and upwards through his legs to his partner. Such odd practices add to the fun element of the lesson while at the same time focusing on skill learning.

Whole body agility can be improved by using a ball with a partner in such activities as *over and under*. The students stand back to back; one bends down to pass the ball backwards through his legs to his partner who takes it and lifts it up over his head to give it back so that the whole process can be repeated. The action can be performed clockwise and anti-clockwise.

In *roundabout* the students again stand back to back and pass the ball around themselves and from one to the other in a clockwise or anti-clockwise direction.

Possibilities for development are, for example, *reach and pass* and *sit up and reach*. *Reach and pass* requires lower back and hamstring flexibility. The students sit back to back, and one starts by holding the ball as far forward as possible between his legs. He then lifts the ball up over his head to his partner who, in turn, reaches forwards. The cycle is then repeated as many times as necessary.

(Top left) Through-the-legs throw-and-catch

(Top right) over . . .

(Below) . . . and Under

Roundabout—the ball can be passed in a clockwise or an anti-clockwise direction

(Below) Reach and pass. One student reaches forwards

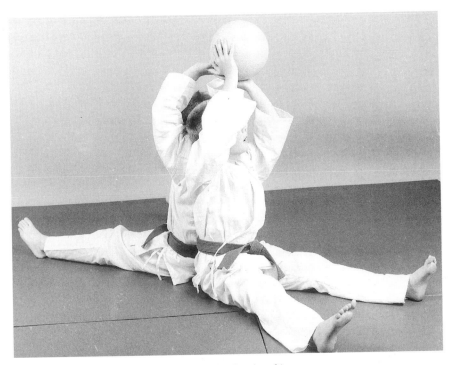

(Above) He sits up and passes the ball overhead to his partner
(Below) His partner then reaches forwards

Sit up and reach. One student lies down, with his arms above his head

Keeping his knees slightly bent, he sits up

He then gives the ball to his partner

The partner in turn lies down

Sit up and reach has a greater effect on the thigh and abdominal muscles and is quite a difficult activity. The students sit feet to feet, and one begins by lying down with the ball held at arm's length behind his head. He then sits up and brings the ball over his head to his partner who proceeds to lie down and sit up in a similar manner. The activity is repeated as often as the coach requests.

A series of team games and relays can be devised using a ball in a similar way to some of the activities already described. For example, in *over the head relay* the students stand in a line; the first person passes the ball over his head to the

Over the head relay

one behind, and so on until the ball reaches the last student who then runs to the front to start the whole action again. Each time the ball reaches the end of the line the last person must run to the front. The winners are the team who get the first person back to the front of the line. Variations include *through the legs*, in which the ball is passed through the legs to the team-mate behind, *over and under*, *pass to the right* and *pass to the left*. The coach must allow his imagination free range to devise activities which are conducive to good skill learning and physical development.

(Above) Kicking with two feet   *(Below) A single-footed kick*

Hamstring curls

The activities outlined so far have concentrated on the upper body and lower back. However, there are some very good practices that can be carried out to develop sound leg action.

Two-footed kicks involve one student lying on his back, with both feet raised and knees bent. A partner carefully throws the ball so that it can be kicked back to him with the soles of the feet.

Single-footed kicks are more demanding than two-footed kicks since greater control is required to kick the ball back with only the right or left foot.

Hamstring curls are an excellent exercise for developing the muscles at the back of the legs. A partner stands over the other, rolling the ball down the back of the legs until it reaches the ankles at which point both heels are flicked back. With practice, the co-ordination of the heel flicks and catching the ball improve markedly.

Seated soccer. Students try to kick the ball to each other with accurate passes

Rolling backwards for an overhead throw

Seated soccer.

The *overhead throw* develops a great deal of co-ordination, albeit in an odd fashion. The student sits on the floor with both legs straight out in front of him and he squeezes the ball between his ankles. He then rolls backwards to flick the ball to his partner who is standing behind.

Simple ways to improve leg strength can also be devised. For example, in *seated soccer* the students face each other and alternately kick the ball with one or both feet to each other. As a variation a medicine ball can be used to increase the load.

THROWING AND CATCHING

Once the young martial artist is happily in control of his own body and of other simple items of equipment an extra dimension can be added to training. At some stage the student will have to come to terms with the fact that he may have to punch someone or, failing that, block a maliciously intended blow. It is essential, therefore, that before he is exposed to such a critical situation he should at least have experienced the rudiments of both actions.

Practices

There are many possible avenues of potential attack or defence. In a very crude fashion I have attempted to identify these various directions in fig. 35. I have kept the picture as uncomplicated as possible and have taken into account attacks from the side or rear. The coach can work out appropriate practices to prepare his student accordingly.

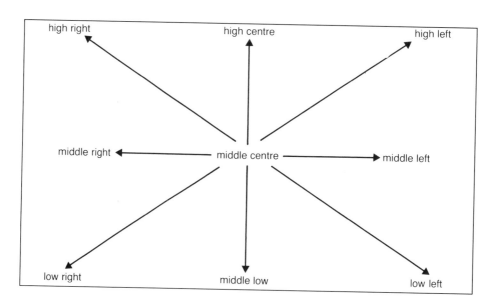

Fig. 35   The 'directional cross' for the development of specific martial arts skills.

In its basic form a punch's movement pattern is similar to that of throwing. So, any youngster who has practised throwing will obviously have an advantage when he later learns the various punching techniques in martial arts. Generally speaking, this is why children who have played such games as cricket pick up punching skills quicker than those who have not.

For these activities it would be best for students to work in pairs. Balls or bean bags are ideal, but coaches should ensure that whichever is used is not too big for the students' hands. Each student throws to his partner from the starting point identified and works systematically through the different actions. The first activity requires the ball to be thrown with both hands, beginning at high right, moving to high centre and high left, progressing through middle left, middle centre and middle right, and finally concluding with low left, middle low and low right. Each time the ball is targeted for the partner to catch. Once the student has been through the routine, it is then repeated but this time he should use either his right hand or his left hand.

Grab ball. The two students each try to wrestle the ball away from their partner

Roller ball. Sitting in an astride position, the student tries to roll the ball around himself, keeping it as far away from his body as possible

Figure-of-eight dribble. The ball is passed around and between the legs in a figure-of-eight shape

Overhead throw. The ball is held in both hands behind the back. It is flicked forwards over the head and is caught in front of the body

A two-handed catch to high right　　*A two-handed catch to high centre*

It is obvious that there should be parallel development of catching skills, because any throwing activities are going to be fraught with difficulties if students cannot catch! However, there is a very important element in what appears to be such a simple skill. Through catching, the young students are able to work out the direction from which the ball is coming and its speed. This, of course, is the basic information which they will need later on when they attempt to apply the correct technique to a punch or kick aimed at them.

A two-handed catch to high left

Catching games should include the same sequence of movements as in the throwing activities, starting at high right and progressing through the different points. Once again, the routine can be started with students using both hands and then made more difficult by requiring the youngsters to use either their left or right hand. (A *two-handed catch* at high right, high centre and high left is illustrated here.)

A catch with the right hand to high right   *A catch with the right hand to high centre*

When the students start to catch with one hand an interesting 'embryonic' technique begins to creep in! In the photographs below we see the normal catching programme using the right hand: catch high right followed by catch high centre. However, when the student moves to catch high left, he will find it easier if he steps across with his right foot. In fact, all catches on the left side—

A right-handed catch to high left. Note how the student steps across to take the catch

A catch with the left hand to left middle

high, middle or low—will require such a movement of the right foot. A similar situation will arise when he progresses to his left hand. Catching to the middle left and centre poses no problems, but as soon as the ball moves across to the right then no matter at what height it is the student will find it easier to step across with his left foot. (See photographs overleaf.)

A catch with the left hand to middle centre

A left-handed catch to middle right

PUNCHING AND BLOCKING

For a student to punch correctly he will need a good pattern of movement. This can be refined through various throwing drills. The ability to work out a target's direction and speed of movement will improve with catching practices. In other words, by practising throwing and catching skills, students will lay down a sound foundation for the next level of skill development.

Practices

For the next series of activities, once again, it is best if the students work in pairs using a ball and working through the various directional points from high right to low left. The same routine of starting with both hands and then only using the right and left can be continued.

The photograph overleaf illustrating two-handed techniques shows the student hitting the ball with both hands high right. The progression continues to high centre; the student may attempt to strike high left, followed by punches to middle right, middle centre and middle left. He may then work at the low level. The coach has to identify specific aspects of technique which may be appropriate to his particular martial art or style.

When the student progresses further to using only one hand there is possibly more opportunity for the coach to give some technical input. However, the degree of technical competence which a coach is seeking must be appropriate to the skill and physical development level of the individual.

Punches with the right hand to high right and to high centre typify the kind of action that is required. However, when the student is using his right hand to punch on his left side he will naturally find it easier to step across with his right foot and hit the ball with the back of his hand. A very crude backfist technique will begin to evolve. (This might be an appropriate moment for the coach to introduce particular aspects of technique.) The same technical modification will happen when the student is using his left hand to strike to the right side: it will be easier to step across with the left foot to use the backfist.

The photograph on page 121 (right) shows a punch to middle right using the right hand. An embryonic reverse punch is emerging at this stage. Without wishing to labour the point, it should be clear by now that the striking technique can be modified by the coach so that those very specific movements of a particular martial art can be mirrored in this simple activity.

A two-handed punch to high right   *A two-handed punch to high centre*

A two-handed punch to middle right

A two-handed punch to high left

A two-handed punch to middle left

A two-handed punch to middle centre

A right-handed punch to high right

A right-handed punch to high centre

The emergence of a basic backfist technique   *A right-handed punch to middle right*

Being able to work out quickly the speed and direction of a blow is obviously a skill which is improved during the catching drills in which the student has to deal with balls coming at him from all angles. Refinement of this skill will lead on to effective blocking. The routine is exactly the same as for punching.

The student starts with both hands. He executes a cross block and waits to block the ball at high right (see the left photograph opposite). As before, he will block at high centre and left and continue to work through the points. The second photograph shows how this blocking practice can be effective as the student successfully blocks a ball from middle centre.

A cross block   *An effective block to middle centre*

When the student moves on to blocking with only one arm the potential for skill development increases. The left photograph on page 126 illustrates the use of the right arm. Here the student is fending off the ball at high centre using a rising block action. The second photograph illustrates a block at middle centre and the third shows that the same techniques can be practised with the left hand. Of course, there are a variety of other blocking techniques. The coach can exercise his judgement as to the type of blocks practised so that in time all can be developed in this simple fashion.

A right-hand rising block to high centre

A right-hand rising block to middle centre

The left hand can be just as effective as the right hand in blocking

Alternative blocks with the left hand . . .

. . . and with the right hand

KICKING

At the start of the section on throwing and catching I pointed out that those children who play ball games involving these two skills usually acquire related martial arts skills quite quickly. I further intimated that it was because of this advantage that they developed punching techniques easier than their peers who

Right knee to high right *Right knee to high centre*

had not played cricket, etc. I would suggest that the same is true of kicking activities, too. Through taking part in rugby, and particularly soccer, young students are going to develop those movement patterns for kicking which are very similar to the basic martial arts techniques.

Practices

Once again, the students practise in pairs with a ball. They work around the directional points, but use only their right or left leg separately. (If some martial arts require double-footed techniques then, of course, they can be added.) I have broken the kicking technique into two elements: using the knee, and using the foot.

When using the knee the same directional points are followed, but obviously the heights are somewhat lower than when punching or blocking. The left photograph on the previous page shows the ball being struck by the knee at high right. There is a whole series of techniques which require the knee to be in this position as a prerequisite to the kicking action. The second photograph shows the right knee at high centre, while the third photograph (below, left)

Left knee to high left   *Right leg to right middle*

Left knee to left middle

Forward action of the knee

Upward action of the knee

A right leg kick to middle right   *A right leg kick to middle centre*

shows the left knee being used at high left. From a coaching point of view it is interesting to note the difference in the range of hip mobility between right and left leg techniques. This could account for technical problems later on if the coach is not aware of difficulties at an early stage. Also illustrated in the photographs are the left knee at left middle, and a similar action with the right leg. Students can also emphasise driving the knee either upwards or forwards. Such a variation in the direction of the force of the knee will have to be considered by the coach who may wish to progress to a specific technique.

Kicking practices with the feet can follow the same pattern, although the ball can be thrown much higher. The coach should specify which part of the foot should be used, ensuring that the action mirrors good technique. The above photographs show a kick to middle right and to middle centre.

VARIATIONS ON A THEME

Once the basic movement patterns have been established they can be refined more and more into martial art-like actions. As already outlined, this can be done initially through identified practices so that at least at first the student has an idea of the feel of a technique. Standard lesson organisation of individual practice in lines and/or working with a partner will further develop the quality of technique.

The questions a coach has to ask himself when faced with juniors is how technically sound are they and can they work safely with a partner in any sparring situation? The reason for this is that a mistimed kick or a poorly performed technique could be dangerous to both the 'attacker' and 'defender' alike. Similarly, a mistimed or poorly executed block could have the same disastrous consequences. The drills and practices so far mentioned go a long way to help the coach assess the stage of a student's development. However, there are further practices which could be equally useful.

Tackle bag

Most clubs have the use of punch pads and bags of various styles which can be an invaluable asset to a coach when assessing the technique of a student against a 'passive' opponent. Through my activities in other sports I have come across a 'Rugby tackle bag' which, I believe, could prove to be a wonderful aid for the imaginative coach. It has several advantages. Firstly, it allows a student to practise a technique without fear of hurting his opponent and, importantly for the 'timid' student, it will not fight back! Secondly, the degree of resistance which the bag offers can be adjusted by the partner. He can hold the bag firmly or can let it go with the gentlest of blows. Thirdly, it is the same height as most juniors and so gives them a sense of scale. By relating it to their own bodies they can see where kicks and punches should be aimed (perhaps a body outline could be painted on it to give a more accurate frame of reference).

The tackle bag can also be invaluable for those martial artists who practise throwing or tripping techniques. Many injuries occur with these activities because a poorly executed technique or breakfall leads to a failure to land safely. The photograph below shows how this problem can be easily resolved through using the bag.

The use of a 'tackle bag' to develop punching techniques

There are several advantages to this practice. Firstly, the bag can be weighted to suit the student's strength so that there is no problem in performing the lifting or tripping element. Secondly, the student can throw the bag as often as he likes, with no complaints from his partner! Thirdly, no competitive stress is placed upon the student; he is not intimidated by his opponent and so his skill should not be affected. Fourthly, taking all these aspects into consideration, the student's only concern is the correct application of technique. Having tried the activity with juniors it was discovered that by 'dressing' the bag with an old gi each student could get a firm hold for whichever technique was being attempted.

Practising roundhouse kicks

Front kicks can also be perfected through use of the tackle bag

A well-executed hip throw

Sweeping moves, as well as throws, can be practised, too. If a partner holds the bag from behind, any leg or foot can be used with the appropriate hold to sweep the base of the floor and complete the technique. Sacrifice and stomach throws can be performed in a similar fashion. In fact, with ingenuity, and ensuring that practices reflect good technique, there are no limits to how this equipment can be used.

INTRODUCTION TO WEAPONS

Many martial arts use weapons. Following the pattern of the previous section, the directional cross can be used to great effect to reproduce safely the basic weapons movement patterns. Many techniques can also be introduced by working in pairs with a bat and ball.

A two-handed strike to high right

A two-handed strike to high centre

A two-handed strike to high left

Techniques which require both hands are easily developed. The photographs above show respectively a technique to high right, to high centre, and to high left. Note once again that the right-handed student steps across with the right foot when applying techniques on the left side. If specific aspects of technique such as the grip or stance need to be highlighted then the coach must do this during the practice.

A right-handed strike to high right

A right-handed strike to middle left

Many techniques use only one hand and again the rudiments of the action can be developed. Using the right hand, the left photograph above shows a strike to high right, while the second photograph shows a modified technique to middle left. The left hand can be used but it is more difficult for the right-handed. The size and shape of the bats can be adjusted to suit the skill level of the student.

There is a further progression for those students who use two weapons such as sai or tonfa at the same time. Once again the coach can identify the specific technical points which he wants the student to develop.

A left-handed strike to middle right

TRAINING DEVELOPMENTS

Thus far the various sections covering aspects of technique have considered the development of the directional cross in a formal fashion. However, once a student has mastered the basics of the technique a form of free practice can be tried. Instead of the student knowing and preparing for a particular kick or punch in a given direction, the coach or partner can mirror the real world by throwing the ball to any point. Over a period of time this will help the student to read direction and speed of movement and to move accordingly. Furthermore, one practice might involve allowing the student to punch, kick or block as he sees fit or as the coach or partner demands.

While all of these practices require the use of only the simplest of equipment—mainly a ball, bean bag, bat or large tackle bag—nevertheless they are sufficient to help the student develop the elementary movement patterns of most martial art techniques. But there is an extra dimension to all these practices for the 'mature' student; if the sponge ball is replaced by a medicine ball then the very same practices can prove to be very useful training aids for the advanced student. (However, I would not advise the use of a medicine ball with students under the age of at least 18.)

TESTING AND MEASURING

As was pointed out earlier, the aim of the various activities and practices described is to give the student a thorough grounding in the rudiments of movement patterns which could be modified later to apply to actual martial arts techniques. In fact as the student improves some of the activities can be altered to mirror specific actions. The current grading systems do not apply as the very nature of these activities is determined by an introduction to and practice of general movement patterns. In reality these drills and practices are a downward extension of the grading system.

It is best to begin by learning the progressive movement patterns in a systematic fashion which is in keeping with the intellectual and physical development of the young student. The student's skills will increase in their complexity as his ability to respond improves, and after this thorough grounding the student will then enter the traditional grading system appropriate to his particular martial art.

The assessment lists in Appendix A are designed to give the coach some record or understanding of the individual's rate of progress. They operate quite simply, with the student working through the list of activities and the coach making some judgement as to the quality of movement at that time. Alternatively, the coach may 'pass' the student as he attains a sufficiently high standard of performance in each activity, use a combination of the two methods or simply use the programmes as ideas for drills.

Whichever way they are used, the assessment lists will provide a record of the elemental skill level of a student. They could also be used diagnostically to try to determine weaknesses in the technique of mature students. Thus, for example, if a student cannot catch a ball it is likely that he will have some difficulty protecting himself from kicks and punches and problems with practising the drills at high, middle or low level or possibly on the right- or the left-hand side might identify where the problems are rooted. Complex techniques cannot be performed at the highest level without a sound foundation of generally related movement patterns.

When using these tables:

- tick off the activities in which the student attains an acceptable skill level.
- use the tables at regular intervals and make a note of the quality of movement.
- use them also as a basis for class activities.

The imaginative coach should be able to devise similar activities much more specific to his own martial art and the needs of his students.

SAFE COACHING

'Years of training indicate neither ability nor experience.' Just because a coach has a black belt does not immediately mean that he is competent. There is a great difference between being a student and having the personal skills to achieve excellence as a coach. The grading structure of most martial arts is geared towards the development of personal standards of competence and technical excellence. Few have a programme designed to educate potential coaches how to teach.

The Martial Arts Commission of Great Britain, in conjunction with the main governing bodies and associations, has produced a comprehensive Coach Education Programme to allow coaches to cross over from student to teacher. Efficient, effective and safe instruction relevant to age, sex and ability of individual students is the main emphasis of the programme. Obviously coaches of young martial artists require all this, together with an in-depth understanding of the problems of teaching lower age groups. They need to know about physical and psychological differences between juniors and adults, as well as have an appreciation that positive coaching of youngsters will produce those students who stay with the activity through their lives. Martial arts presented in the correct way will ensure the success not just of the individual club and coach but of the activity in general.

The M.A.C Coach Education programme is divided into several categories: Assistant Club Coach, Club Coach and Senior Coach. More details of these courses can be obtained from the M.A.C, but briefly the requirements are as follows.

All potential candidates must be recommended by their governing body, be over eighteen years of age and hold a recognised First Aid qualification. The courses each comprise a series of lectures, seminars and practical assessments.

Assistant coach award

This covers the following:

- what does the coach do?
- how does the coach behave?
- the coach's responsibility

- how to coach
- how to screen new students
- training safety
- the whys and wherefores of warm-up and cool-down
- coaching and the law
- how to deal with emergencies
- where the club and coach fit into the national Martial Arts structure.

Club coach award

The normal candidate for this award will have been an Assistant Coach for some time before being recommended by his association. The topics covered are:

- how to get the best from your students
- how to measure students' progress
- how to improve students' fitness
- how to counsel students over training set-backs
- how to rehabilitate injured students
- how to coach young children
- how to set targets and plan training
- how to start a new club
- managing a club
- organising courses and events.

The culmination of this award is a practical assessment of coaching proficiency.

Senior coach award

The potential candidates are those individuals who have a wealth of teaching experience and who have been identified by their governing body. They should also have a proven track record as coaches. At this level there will be major differences in course content and requirements for the various martial arts associations. Close involvement with the M.A.C. is required to produce a custom-made package that is specific to each martial art or style. However, topics that are usually covered are as follows:

- communication skills
- stress control techniques
- mechanics of sport
- working with teams

■ peak performance
■ competitive sport and young children
■ sports injury prevention and care.

There are further awards for the most senior coaches, those of Coach Tutor and Principal Coaching Officer. Since they are highly specific, these courses are run in close co-operation with the M.A.C. so that the demands of individual organisations can be met.

This Coach Education Programme has been carefully designed to cater for the majority of martial arts in Britain and to bring coaching into line with other sports and activities. However, should the packages identified not meet with the specific requirements of an association, then members can use the National Coaching Foundation courses instead. Full details of these can be obtained from the N.C.F. or the M.A.C.

INSURANCE

'He who would be his own lawyer has got a fool for a client.'

It is essential that every student, coach, club and governing body or association is fully covered by the appropriate insurance. The Martial Arts Commission organises a comprehensive series of policies to cover all aspects of training and competition. Queries regarding the policies, their terms and conditions should be referred to the M.A.C. However, briefly these fall into the following categories.

Student to student cover

This policy provides cover against personal accident and the risk of injuring others. The M.A.C. licence application form must be completed before any martial arts training commences. Basically, students are covered against any injury which might arise from training with a fellow student.

Professional indemnity

Anybody who is teaching, coaching, instructing or training students in the martial arts must have the appropriate cover. It should be remembered that when instruction is being given by an individual, the normal student to student cover lapses.

There is no differentiation in law between a professional and an amateur coach. Professional indemnity cover must be acquired by both, and this includes assistant, club and senior coaches. Other high-grade students who are asked to take groups, particularly beginners, should ensure they are covered.

Dental cover

Should any injury lead to dental damage, cost of treatment is covered.

Club liability

There are two further areas which should also be considered: the building in which training takes place, and the building's contents, including students' possessions.

It is essential that all concerned are fully aware of their legal responsibilities in the unfortunate instance of an accident. I cannot recommend too strongly that both parents and coaches ask for advice from the M.A.C. and/or their governing bodies and associations. For the caring club and coach it might, in fact, be a promotional feature that all tuition is given by fully qualified instructors in receipt of a nationally recognised coaching award and having comprehensive insurance cover. It is not good practice to be wise after the event.

GOOD PRACTICE

Since over 60% of students are between the ages of 6 and 16 years, it follows that they will make up the bulk of new students joining clubs. So, what precautions should be taken to ensure their continued safety and progress in their chosen activity?

It is recommended that any new student joining a club should be screened. The demands of a martial art are both physically and mentally high, and each student must be capable of withstanding the pressures. It is the responsibility of the coach to protect youngsters from work which is beyond their capacity. An interview with the potential student and parent is not only good practice but also reassures caring parents that they are leaving their child in the hands of a caring coach.

I would suggest that at an initial interview a series of questions are put to the parent and child with the answers being noted down on a questionnaire-type form for future reference (see Appendix B). I have drafted an example of the type of information which I would consider useful, but individual coaches might want to add to or remove some of the questions. Basically, what you need to know is that the student is in good health and is able to practise martial arts. Any condition that might affect either his own safety or that of the other students must be noted. If the coach then decides that there is a problem he should consult a doctor to ensure that it is safe for the potential student to train. Once this has been done it is essential that a parent or a guardian signs the form to signify that the information given is correct.

Although they may have read about or seen coverage of the martial arts on the television, many people do not appreciate fully what is involved in martial arts training. Once the initial interview with parent and child has taken place it is essential that they watch at least two lessons to see what actually goes on. Some parents might decide after viewing a lesson that it is not what they thought it was and that it is too hazardous for their child. Nevertheless it is essential that parents are aware of the nature of martial arts training before they give their permission for their child to practise.

There is a moral and legal obligation placed on the coach that any young student should leave the training area in the same condition as he came in! Parents who are not aware of the demands of the activity can become quite concerned with small cuts and bruises appearing on their angelic children. The coach thus has the responsibility of acting 'in loco parentis', which basically means acting towards a child in the same way as any caring parent would. This can prove to be more of a problem than at first appears because, due to their immaturity, young students cannot be expected to show great self-discipline and control when it comes to using techniques which they have learned.

LEGAL IMPLICATIONS

Quality of instruction is not the sole requirement of a coach in the martial arts. There are also legal implications for every facet of teaching which are even more important when coaching young students.

It is not my intention to cover the law as it relates to the teaching of martial arts—that would require a book in its own right. However, the following sections seek to give coaches an understanding of the main aspects involved.

Before the lesson begins the coach must, as a matter of habit, ensure that students are not wearing any jewellery which might cause injury to themselves or to others. All nails should be well manicured, not just to prevent them breaking but, more importantly, so that they do not cause harm to delicate areas such as the eyes. It is also very important to wear the correct type of clothing for the particular martial art being practised. This might prove difficult with new students, but a successful club should be able to lend essential items until such time as the student has acquired his own.

Training area

The training area must have sufficient floor space to allow students to practise without colliding or landing on top of each other. The minimum recommended floor or mat size is 5.5 metres × 5.5 metres or 7 metres × 5 metres. Obviously, the larger the area, the better. For basic individual practice it is recommended that each student should have 3 square metres of space. Kata activity requires 4 square metres while randori or free practice needs 11 square metres for each pair. Too many students on the mat at any one time is very dangerous and in the event of an accident the coach would be deemed responsible. The successful coach can resolve the problem in a variety of ways.

- *Shorter lessons* These will keep the interest of the students and will prevent them from becoming bored. Also, the shorter the time, the more lessons that can be taught. The advantage of this strategy is that the smaller numbers allow the coach to pay more attention to each student.
- *Teaching style* By carefully designing the lesson around sections of time (for example kicking techniques for ten minutes followed by punching

techniques), the coach can split the group into two, with one group on the mat while the other group watches and rests. The advantage of this system is that the students can reinforce their skill learning by carefully watching others. Looking at good and bad technique and discussing the quality of movement is just as important in skill development as mat time.

Floor condition

The condition of the floor is just as important as its dimensions. Where a hard floor is used it must be clean and free from any protruding or damaged floorboards or tiles. A good grip is required for the feet to prevent slipping. The floor area must be kept clear at all times and the coach should watch out for bags, belts, weapons or any other item which could cause a student to trip. Techniques such as throws, take-downs or even breakfalls should not be taught on a hard surface as young students are very vulnerable.

Where mats are used their condition is equally crucial. There must be no tears of damage either to their surface or to their filling. They must not slide apart during a lesson and the coach must watch for this constantly. A student could turn or twist an ankle easily by stepping into the gap between mats, and if this happened during the application of a technique there could be damage to one or both of the students involved. Similarly, falling on to an unprotected floor area is potentially very dangerous. The type of mat used is also significant. Make certain that only mats manufactured specifically for the requirements of your martial art are used. Any old mat found lying around will not do. If such a mat is used and injury occurs due to inadequate 'cushioning', the coach may be liable. Coaches who use other peoples' matting, for example, in a sports centre, should take special care.

Building

The building itself must also be safe to use. There should be no unprotected glass windows or doors within three metres of the training area. The amount of lighting is crucial, particularly for weapons work, since the students must be able to see. It is vital that, for weapons work, there is sufficient clearance for their use without shattering fluorescent light tubes all over the floor! It is recommended that there should be at least 3 metres from the floor to the ceiling or to any fixtures and fittings. Any pillars, radiators or other objects which might be dangerous must be covered with sufficient padding. Mirrors, which are an excellent training aid, should be kept away from the general training area just in case!

Equipment

Items of equipment such as weapons, protective clothing, kick or punch pads, punch bags and medicine balls must be maintained on a regular basis and must be checked by the coach prior to use each and every session. A young student does not have the knowledge to identify any wear and tear or other dangerous signs.

Spectators

Most students at some time will bring along their parents or a friend to watch. Any spectators must be kept at least three metres away from the action but ideally more. For gradings and competitions you should make sure that the area around the mat does not get overcrowded.

There are some very important new legal requirements with respect to both organised events and the safety of spectators. Basically, any activity to which spectators are invited, including parents watching a club session, needs a licence from the local authority. The statute to which this applies comes under the heading of 'The Fire Safety and Safety of Places of Sport Act 1987' (Part IV—Indoor Sports Licences). If you hold your lessons in a local authority run sports facility you may already be covered by its certificate, but you should check. Otherwise, consult your local Fire Prevention Officer and your local authority Safety Officer. They will advise you on the relevant regulations and, if necessary, tell you the procedures you need to go through.

Access

Access to and from the training hall has to be adequate. There must be lighting both on the stairs and at the entry points outside as well as inside all the facilities, particularly in winter. When dealing with young martial artists no chances can be taken with their safety. Thus adequate ventilation and heating must be provided, both for reasons of hygiene and for comfortable and safe training, because it is dangerous to train in an area which is either too cold or too hot. Security is important not just for the building but also for the belongings of the students while they train—valuables and clothing have a habit of 'disappearing' if not looked after.

Injuries

A first-aid kit should be readily available in case of minor injuries such as cuts, damaged nails or the occasional graze. It is essential that the contents of this kit are regularly checked and replaced. You should know where the nearest hospital with a casualty department is should there be an injury which requires further medical attention. This is particularly important in those areas where hospitals work together according to a rota to provide cover. Depending on the nature of the injury it might be totally inappropriate to transport a student to hospital by car, and therefore it is essential that the coach has ready access to a telephone for a '999' call.

Equally important in the case of any injury is an accident record book. It is essential for both the student and the coach that the exact injury, how it occurred and the treatment administered should be noted. The age of the student, the time of the accident, the number of students in the class and the names of those present at the incident might also be recorded. There can never be too much information, particularly if a claim is made at a later date when the memory has faded. The only alternative is to video tape each lesson!

If the emphasis is placed on safety in this way the caring coach should have no difficulties with the legal implications arising from accidents. Some coaches may find these requirements too demanding, but for the safe training of students, especially young ones who don't have the experience or the knowledge to recognise a dangerous situation, no precaution can be too much trouble.

APPENDIX A

Assessment check-lists

General movement

Guerrilla crawl
Hands and knees crawl
Seal walk
Crouch walk
Bear walk
Walking
Running
Stopping both feet
Stopping one foot
Hopping
Stepping
Run, jump, land
Take off right foot, land both feet
Take off right foot, land right foot
Take off right foot, land left foot
Take off left foot, land both feet
Take off left foot, land left foot
Take off left foot, land right foot
Run, jump, stretch, land
Run, jump, tuck, land
Run, jump, half-turn, land
Run, jump, full turn, land
Continuous hopping left foot
Continuous hopping right foot
Continuous stepping
Continuous Bunny Jumps

Rolling

Kipper roll left
Kipper roll right
Forward roll
Backward roll
Side roll left
Side roll right
Diagonal roll front left
Diagonal roll back right
Diagonal roll front right
Diagonal roll back left
Kata of rolls
Rolls from crouch position
Rolls from half-squat position
Rolls from standing
Dive rolls

Throwing

Throw both hands high right
Throw both hands high centre
Throw both hands high left
Throw both hands mid-section right
Throw both hands mid-section centre
Throw both hands mid-section left
Throw both hands low right
Throw both hands low centre
Throw both hands low right
Throw high right, right hand
Throw high centre, right hand
Throw high left, right hand
Throw mid-section right, right hand
Throw mid-section centre, right hand
Throw mid-section left, right hand
Throw low left, right hand
Throw low centre, right hand
Throw low left, right hand
Throw high right, left hand
Throw high centre, left hand

Throw high left, left hand
Throw mid-section right, left hand
Throw mid-section centre, left hand
Throw mid-section left, left hand
Throw low right, left hand
Throw low centre, left hand
Throw low right, left hand

Catching

Catch both hands high right
Catch both hands high centre
Catch both hands high left
Catch both hands mid-section right
Catch both hands mid-section centre
Catch both hands mid-section left
Catch both hands low right
Catch both hands low centre
Catch both hands low right
Catch high right, right hand
Catch high centre, right hand
Catch high left, right hand
Catch mid-section right, right hand
Catch mid-section centre, right hand
Catch mid-section left, right hand
Catch low left, right hand
Catch low centre, right hand
Catch low left, right hand
Catch high right, right hand
Catch high centre, left hand
Catch high left, left hand
Catch mid-section right, left hand
Catch mid-section centre, left hand
Catch mid-section left, left hand
Catch low right, left hand
Catch low centre, left hand
Catch low right, left hand

Punching

Punch both hands high right
Punch both hands high centre
Punch both hands high left
Punch both hands mid-section right
Punch both hands mid-section centre
Punch both hands mid-section left
Punch both hands low right
Punch both hands low centre
Punch both hands low right

Punch high left, right hand
Punch high centre, right hand
Punch high left, right hand
Punch mid-section right, right hand
Punch mid-section centre, right hand
Punch mid-section left, right hand
Punch low right, right hand
Punch low centre, right hand
Punch low left, right hand
Punch high right, left hand
Punch high centre, left hand
Punch high left, left hand
Punch mid-section right, left hand
Punch mid-section centre, left hand
Punch mid-section left, left hand
Punch low right, left hand
Punch low centre, left hand
Punch low right, left hand

Blocking

Block both hands high right
Block both hands high centre
Block both hands high left
Block both hands mid-section right
Block both hands mid-section centre
Block both hands mid-section left
Block both hands low right
Block both hands low centre
Block both hands low left
Block high right, right hand
Block high centre, right hand
Block high left, right hand
Block mid-section right, right hand
Block mid-section centre, right hand
Block mid-section left, right hand
Block low right, right hand
Block low centre, right hand
Block low left, right hand
Block high right, left hand
Block high centre, left hand
Block high left, left hand
Block mid-section right, left hand
Block mid-section centre, left hand
Block mid-section left, left hand
Block low right, left hand
Block low centre, left hand
Block low right, left hand

Kicking

Kick high right, right foot
Kick high centre, right foot
Kick high left, right foot
Kick mid-section right, right foot
Kick mid-section centre, right foot
Kick mid-section left, right foot
Kick low right, right foot
Kick low centre, right foot
Kick low left, right foot
Kick high right, left foot
Kick high centre, left foot
Kick high left, left foot
Kick mid-section right, left foot
Kick mid-section centre, left foot
Kick mid-section left, left foot
Kick low right, left foot
Kick low centre, left foot
Kick low left, left foot

'Kneeing'

Knee high right, right knee
Knee high centre, right knee
Knee high left, right knee
Knee mid-section right, right knee
Knee mid-section centre, right knee
Knee mid-section left, right knee
Knee low left, right knee
Knee low centre, right knee
Knee low left, right knee
Knee high right, left knee
Knee high centre, left knee
Knee high left, left knee
Knee mid-section right, left knee
Knee mid-section centre, left knee
Knee mid-section left, left knee
Knee low right, left knee
Knee low centre, left knee
Knee low left, left knee

Throwing

Straight lift

Hip throw—right
Hip throw—left
Right-foot sweep de ashi harai
Left-foot sweep
Right leg major outer reaping o soto gari
Left leg major outer reaping
Right leg major inner reaping o uchi gari
Left leg major inner reaping
Right shoulder throw seoi nage
Left shoulder throw
Right side body drop tai toshi
Left side body drop

Batting

Bat both hands high right
Bat both hands high centre
Bat both hands high left
Bat both hands mid-section right
Bat both hands mid-section centre
Bat both hands mid-section left
Bat both hands low right
Bat both hands low centre
Bat both hands low right
Bat high right, right hand
Bat high centre, right hand
Bat high left, right hand
Bat mid-section right, right hand
Bat mid-section centre, right hand
Bat mid-section left, right hand
Bat low left, right hand
Bat low centre, right hand
Bat low left, right hand
Bat high right, left hand
Bat high centre, left hand
Bat high left, left hand
Bat mid-section right, left hand
Bat mid-section centre, left hand
Bat mid-section left, left hand
Bat low right, left hand
Bat low centre, left hand
Bat low left, left hand

Appendix B

Parents' questionnaire

Surname ....

Forename(s) ....

Date of Birth ....

Telephone number ....

School ....

Previous experience in martial arts ....

....

M.A.C. licence number ....

Date of issue ....

Medical History
Approval of G.P. .... Yes/No

Please tick if you suffer from any of the following.

Diabetes	Epilepsy ....
Migraine	Haemophilia ....
Heart Disorders	Respiratory Disorders ....
Joint Pains	Allergies ....

Any other difficulties ....

....

Reasons for practising martial arts ....

....

(continued overleaf)

I give permission for my son/daughter to train in the martial arts, and accept that by the nature of the activity there may be a risk of injury.

Signature of Parent or Guardian ....

Date ....

The governing body and the associated club reserve the right to decline your application and revoke your authority to train should your safety and that of other students become at risk.

INDEX